Handbook of
Venusian Spirituality

Handbook of Venusian Spirituality
Omnec Onec

Copyright © 2023 DISCUS Publishing, Anja Schäfer

This publication is the only authorized version from Omnec Onec.

DISCUS
PUBLISHING

For permission requests send an email to info@discuspublishing.com.

Publisher's Website: *https://discuspublishing.com*

Cover Mandala: Iris Merlino

Layout: Anja Schäfer

ISBN: 978-3-910804-11-1

OMNEC ONEC

HANDBOOK

OF

VENUSIAN

SPIRITUALITY

Table of Contents

Preface from the Publisher

*T*his little book pearl was already written at the end of the nineties. With this edition, it is now published for the first time in English in its original, complete form, as Omnec wrote it back then.

A few words about the background: After the first publication of Omnec Onec's autobiography "From Venus I Came" in 1991 in the USA, her soul mission led her directly to the German-speaking world. From the interest of people who had experienced Omnec live in public appearances and who were deeply touched by her unique autobiography about her life on the astral plane of Venus, a great desire arose for more knowledge on how to apply the spiritual teachings of the Venusians into everyday life.

As a consequence, two more books were written, which were available for a long period in German only: her autobiography part 2 with the title "Angels Don't Cry" as well as this "Handbook of Venusian Spirituality".

May this small, pure pearl of love and wisdom remind you of your divine being as a beloved soul and be a compass for you on your way home.

Universal love and blessings

Anja Schäfer

Acknowledgement

I This book is dedicated to my publishers along with many families and friends who welcomed me into their hearts and homes. Also to all who helped me with this book by lending me their ears, listening to my ideas and contributing with ideas, so I may better understand the needs of all beings; also to those higher beings who channeled information from their levels; to uncle Odin who formulated some mantras and who's humor helped me.

Thank all of you my ever growing families for your support and love helping me to not feel like a stranger in your world.

My hope is that this be valuable information to create whole, balanced, powerful souls with a greater understanding of themselves and all the wonders and endless possibilities of the creation of which we are all a part. May I be an inspiration on behalf of my fellow Venusians and all great beings that I represent.

Amual Abaktu Baraka Bashad

(Universal love and blessings)

Omnec

Image 1: Omnec Onec, 1994

Introduction

$\mathcal{T}$he Handbook of Venusian Spirituality is made up of our Venusian concepts of ourselves in relation to the world around us and the other existing dimensions above or below us or as we like to understand all around us. It gives you our view of every living entity from a soul point of view. It is a guide to help you not only understand but balance and harmonize all the non-material bodies within the physical body. It is a step-by-step guide of how to properly care for the physical, astral, causal, mental, etheric, and soul bodies.

It has exercises – physical and others. It also sets programs to replace misinformation. Further it gives you guidelines to help you recognize your progress. It has mantras for morning, afternoon and night, also mantras for each existing dimension and meditation procedures for each.

Also in this handbook are never before published Venusian ceremonies, for which I have received the permission to make them public. These you may try and enjoy yourselves.

I as a former astral being have set the following guidelines to help you absorb and properly understand what lies in the following pages. This information is based on my experiences here on Earth and what I brought with me from Venus. Much of the information is also based on the needs I have encountered in my relationships here on Earth and especially what I have learned through media encounters and workshops. My life as well is a great learning experience for me as an individual, and as I learn I try to share with all I can.

Since entering into the physical body I have found of course that in this material world you encounter limits as it is on each dimension. For each dimension of existence has spiritual laws that govern the extent of what we can or cannot experience in that particular existence or dimension.

So to my best abilities I try to work within the limits in a most unlimited way so that you may experience as much as possible within your own individual consciousness and physical limitations.

First patience is very important as everything needs time to develop. Also the spiritual bodies need adjustments to new experiences. It is all individual as you each are.

Every experience is not always sensational but sometimes very fine and subtle – we must learn to become sensitive to fine experiences.

A further good preparation for life and for the teachings in this book is a sense of humor. I have found that in the physical world where you cannot always control the conditions that happen or exist that one can try to view it with a sense of humor. It has helped me through many trials. Learn to laugh at yourself and then it does not hurt so much when others laugh at you. After all we are not perfect yet!

Now the first chapter is about the maintenance and care for the physical. I know it is boring but after all we all still have a physical body! Since we reside in the physical we must at least understand it because tolerating it is not sufficient. Because to tolerate is only to accept but not to really care – and we must care about the whole self.

We need the body in order to be able to exist, communicate and move around. You will learn it can be wonderful. I had to learn the hard way, I am trying to make it easier for you. The body is a vehicle for the soul. The soul is the driver, the body the car. Now who wants to drive around in a dirty, beaten up, rusted, broken-down car? Well, read on... We will soon have all of you brilliant inside and out!

Enjoy while you improve!

Chapter 1 – Understanding the Physical

*I*n the Venusian society we have a concept of spirituality as a balancing of one selves on all levels. If one resides in the physical this includes the physical body. You must take care that the physical body is healthy and balanced. Exercise, diet and proper rest are necessary. Further you must accept that the physical body is mostly genetic in structure and many of our physical attributes are inherited. Some of us are tall, short, heavy, muscular, thin etc. by nature. We must be able to work within our own physical limitations and accept them, also to use them to our advantage.

First to accept each of ourselves as unique and individual is a must. To see ourselves as we are and realize the beauty that is individual we must set our own standards and not accept standards set by others. That does not mean that we are perfect and do not need to work on ourselves. It means we need to find what works for us individually.

Everyone can always improve themselves. Even a thin person's muscles can become slack and loose. Being active is important. Walking, climbing stairs, dancing, sports – all can be beneficial. Sometimes we rely to much on automobiles and not on our legs. People who sit a lot at work need more exercises than those who move about at work. Do not enroll in aerobics unless you will enjoy it.

Anything you undertake should be something you will enjoy or you will soon loose interest. I love dancing and I attribute it to myself being able to stay in shape. I am short and slim but would quickly loose my shape if I did not love to walk. I take long walks because I enjoy nature and I love to dance. So half an hour a day I put on music and do outlandish dancing all by myself. By outlandish I mean lying on the floor and waving hands and legs around. Of course everyone may not enjoy this. You have to fit your exercise to yourself and your life style.

Sex is also a very healthy activity. (It helps to have a partner.)

Eating habits are also important. There are plenty of books about diet. However, it is important to not become fanatical about anything. Because then you have upset the balance of your physical self. It is good to be healthy, but not to be a health fanatic. You once again have to make the choice as to what you are comfortable with. If you eliminate meat from your diet, consider that all living things have souls and will one day evolve into the human state! That is correct – all plants, minerals and animals are souls, incarnated in different existences for experiences. When their particular purpose is served in this state they leave the physical and return into a higher state of existence.

So we must choose to eat what benefits us and not worry that we are destroying something. You destroy your own body by overindulgence of any kind. You have to pay attention to how your body feels and responds to different foods. Because we all are different.

I have found that by reducing the starch intake (potatoes, corn, bread, rice, noodles) and of course sugar, can reduce your weight if you are overweight. If you have one helping of starch you do not need two. You do not need bread with noodles, rice, corn or potatoes.

Being vegetarian is good. But to eliminate meat, cheese, eggs, fish all from the diet is not good. You miss the protein that is essential to good health. Remember balance is important. Do not use the way you eat to feel superior to others. It is important to be healthy, not superior. You cannot attain spiritual perfection through diet. However, you can be healthy balanced and above all not judgmental of others in the process of learning. Much better is it to share your information and help others. Remember we are all beautiful souls inside this physical structure. We must try to reflect this in our appearance to the best of our abilities. Believe me, it is easier on the astral when we do not have a physical body. However, most of you reading this have a physical structure!

Now personal dressing or grooming habits are vital. We must care how we appear. It will make you more self-confident if you feel that you look good. I do not mean you have to look like a movie star. But to be well groomed and neat and clean is important – also for those closest to you!

You must not just say appearance does not matter. Of course it does! If you have went around only wearing black don't you think you could brighten your image a little? Find clothes that are comfortable and attractive. Try a few different colors, fall into a new image. Break old habits and discover the hidden you. Do not be afraid to try new ideas. You can always change. But it is essential to be clean.

I really found this first troublesome after I had manifested a physical body. I thought it were a waste of time to bath, brush teeth, change clothes, comb hair. It was a never ending process. Then I realized I felt better if I did and people did not mind coming close to me!

Being creative is another important factor in being physical. It actually helps to stimulate the energy that constantly flows through the body. Unfortunately, many people do not consider themselves as creative. Being creative does not mean you have to be a great artist. It means to find a way to express yourself and your feelings.

You are being creative if you see shapes in the clouds. You are creative if you find a use for something that someone else discarded. You are being creative if you repair something with wire or tape because of necessity. Everything that people have created was out of necessity. They needed something and created it! Because we are attuned to the Creator and are part of that energy that created us we are by nature creators ourselves! We create families, societies, means of travel and communication. Extend this further and focus on the ways you can become more creative. Remember the more you use your creative energy the more creative energy will flow through you.

Fasting Techniques

Fasting one to three days is also helpful for an optimal physical condition. One way if it is physically difficult to fast is to try to be positive and focus on spiritual thoughts for a whole day. Focus on the needs of others or be thankful for all the benefits of your existence. It is always good to bless the souls that have been created to sustain and provide you with nourishment.

One fasting technique is to only eat fruit and fresh vegetables and to drink juice, water, herb teas. Abstain from protein, starch as well from coffee, alcohol, cigarettes etc.

Do a three day fast only if you can rest and not have to do physical or mental or emotional stressing activities. Just relax, listen to music, read a book.

The Ghee-Diet

This is a known yoga diet. It is to thoroughly cleanse the intestinal tract of food wastes that become trapped in the passages and nots. It also rids the body of accumulated toxins. However, I recommend not to do it more than once a year. Also you must have three days free of physical labor where you may rest without any type of stress. I tried it and shall share with you my experience.

You must begin the first morning or night before and prepare the Ghee, which is ½ lb. unsalted pure butter per person. You boil it for one hour on very low heat. It must be warm and melted each time you take it. You take three tablespoons of the Ghee (melted butter) as the first thing upon arising in the morning. Then you may only eat cooked cereal – oats, wheat, barley and grains, except rice. This is all you are allowed to consume, other than juice (unsweetened), water or unsweetened herb tea. No coffee, black tea, alcohol or cigarettes are allowed. You continue the same for three days.

You might experience headaches or mild stomach cramps at first. This assures you that it is working. This is the reaction of the body as it is used to having certain amounts of coffee, black tea, alcohol, coca cola etc. This will pass. You will feel weak and light headed or dizzy. But finally you will notice a clarity of sight, hearing, smell, and the feelings become re-sensitized. You will feel regenerated and have more alertness and energy. This was my experience, of course it will depend on the amount of toxins in the body. Good luck!

Recipe for Ghee

½ lb. unsalted butter, boiled for one hour and heated before each dose of three table spoons at the beginning of each of the three days.

You may choose your own cereal – oats, wheat, barley, etc., but no rice! You may eat as much each day as you wish. No salt, milk or sweetener.

All of these above listed fasts give the bodies and especially the physical body a rest and cleansing.

I view eating meat as an individual choice. If you eat meat three times a day for 15-20 years it is good to cut down or eliminate it most of the time. However, do not become fanatic about it. Sometimes you will feel the need to have it. However, there are those who cannot tolerate certain food. You must learn to eat what benefits you, without guilt. Enjoy what you consume and do not overindulge or consume too much of anything. Be thankful to the souls that once was what you are eating.

Two of my favorite healthy delicious recipes:

The Cellulite Melt

To melt and burn off existing fat deposits – for thin or heavy people

1 bunch celery

1 lb. green beans – fresh if possible or frozen

1 lb. spinach

1 bunch parsley

1 clove garlic

2 liters water

Wash and cut all vegetables about 1-2 inches, chop garlic.

Bring water to boil in a large pot, add spinach, beans, celery, boil five minutes. Turn off heat, add parsley and garlic. Boil five more minutes. Add sea or vegetable salt for taste – or none. (Not too much.)

Blend in blender till soupy. Drink warm or cold a large glass before breakfast and another before lunch, then one at bedtime. This is good to everyday for a week. You may do it every week or once a month for a week! Store in the refrigerator.

Crunchy Space Granola

Can be eaten as a snack dry or with milk or in yoghurt

3 lbs. oats

½ lb. shelled walnuts

½ lb. raisins

¼ lb. sesamee seeds

½ lb. coconut, shredded or chopped

½ lb. almonds, shelled

½ cup brown sugar

1 small jar honey

¼ cup vegetable oil

1 small spoon salt

Mix all ingredients in a large container. You may have to use hands – it is alright, wash them first. You are only putting your love and energy into it which is essential!

When it is not powdery but like a dry cookie dough it is ready.

Spread a nice layer into a baking pan cookie shut or pizza pan which has been coated with oil. Then bake at about 225 till brown. Then turn it all over and brown the rest. Continue until it is all finished. Put it into a large container to cool and store later.

I hope you enjoy these and share it with friends. It is always good!

There are many videos and books for self-help on the market that deal with diets and exercises. Find your best suited procedure and stick to it. (If you cheat once in a while as we all do, do not feel guilty, enjoy the break, but do go back to your system.)

Now on to the emotional self.

Chapter 2 – Learning to deal with the Emotions

$\mathcal{N}$ ow we are getting into a very difficult and sensitive area for all living entities, especially the human being, as many of our emotional experiences result not only from our existence here but some are from previous lifetimes and carried by the soul via memories or experiences.

Emotions are a very essential part of existence for we could not exist without feelings. These relate to every part of our being – how we physically look and feel, how we mentally function to our ability to relate to everyone and everything around us. It is easier to become emotionally unbalanced than almost any other functions, because the emotions are constantly in motion or use.

Life is an emotional roller coaster, constantly changing as our experiences. The emotions take us up from one existence to another.

The dimension that controls and supplies the emotional body is the astral plane. To exist there is to rely on the feelings and experiences and to exist in an emotional state of consciousness. This is fine if you exist on the astral in the astral body. However, it is difficult to rely only on the emotions on the physical as I found out the hard way.

We are supplied with senses to help us relate and experience in the physical. Our senses directly affect us emotionally.

From birth we are affected by touch, taste, sight, sound, and even smells. These senses supply us with our first emotional patterns in this life. Basic emotional patterns are reactions or responses to things around us, such as smiling or laughing when we are content, crying in discomfort or fear. Eventually we progress from basic emotional behavior and create ties or bonds to people or comfort.

As we grow older we also encounter emotional crises and create emotional conflicts in our relationship to people within our daily life. One can even become emotionally addicted to certain behaviors or comforts – even to other people. But then emotional imbalance occurs. Also when we no longer can control our emotional behavior we have an imbalance. Sometimes these occurrences are caused by a physical chemical imbalance. But this is not controllable by normal means.

Emotions have a lot to do with self-confidence – being happy, sad, being able to feel comfortable in strange situations.

Many find that because of some deep emotional traumas they have difficulty when encountering similar situations that caused the trauma. Many spend their lives avoiding such situations and running from these experiences. Sometimes this behavior becomes habitual and one is not aware that they are carrying unnecessary emotional baggage. Some look to drugs, alcohol or some other emotionally stimulating activity as a means of escape. Others are institutionalized as a result of not understanding or being able to cope emotionally. These are chronic cases, but all can be helped.

As the emotional body is a primary important function we should strive to be emotionally well and balanced. Misinformation, mistreatment and a lot of social teachings are directly responsible for many emotionally ill people.

Do not let all that you have just read frighten you into an appointment with a psychotherapist or into doing self-analysis yet. The first step to being emotionally happy and balanced is to be able to understand why you feel like you do. Perhaps it is simply that you are just finding out that you are a soul inhabiting a physical body, and to be able to view yourself this way is a giant step!

It is perfectly normal to become angry in certain situations but not to become overly aggressive. All emotions are usually normal reactions. However, we must not become so emotional that we loose control. It is easy to become emotionally involved or attached. You are your best judge as far as understanding your own emotions. Sometimes in an emotional conflict we should only take a break, step back and examine the situation. When we feel that we are becoming too emotional we must learn to control our own feelings. One of the biggest causes of conflicts is trying to control or force other individuals to see or feel the way we do. To recognize that each person has the right to feel and think from their own perspective changes a lot of conflicting situations to one of understanding and acceptance. Always ask yourself about the way you are reacting emotionally. You may be surprised at how much of it is habit. You may find that you really feel different after all.

A good exercise for the emotions is to make a list of what makes you angry. Then list things that you fear. Then list what makes you comfortable, happy and sad. Try to understand these feelings and why you feel certain ways about certain experiences. Try to overcome your fears. Try to understand the anger. Try to imagine smiling instead of feeling angry.

It also helps to write down a real traumatic emotional situation that deeply affected you. Write it down and you have released it. Then find someone to share it with, someone you trust. You will be surprised at how much relief you feel.

We must all have emotional outlets or something we enjoy doing for relaxing. It is good to also pamper yourself sometimes – a good massage for example. This is always physically and emotionally therapeutic. I like a nice scented bath with candle light, incense and music. Of course meditation is also very good for the emotions. For a special meditation procedure read chapter 8.

You will find that if you can control your emotions you will function better socially and it will do wonders for your career, and of course understanding how you function emotionally does wonders for personal relationships as well.

Personal relationships with family, close friends or a partner rely on you being honest about your feelings and dealing with conflicts as they happen, not letting it build up until there is an overload and then having angry outbursts. If someone says or does something which hurts or upsets you, then you should say so calmly at the moment. Letting people know how you feel is important. If you have a family member or a past friendship that ended in hard feelings it is important to solve this by contacting, writing or talking to them, because you are also carrying this around and it can create a karmic debt or tie that you do not need.

As a more aware person you are responsible for your actions and situations. It is up to you to make the first step to clear up misunderstandings and conflicts. This way you free your-self of this. Even if the other person refuses to accept their part or does not want to discuss it or forgive then you are still free as you have taken the responsibility for your part and made an effort. Then it is only their problem as you have taken care of your involvement. You have freed yourself of the unnecessary emotional baggage and solved your part. You can only be responsible for yourself and do what you know is correct for you and your well-being. You are not responsible for their reaction or lack of understanding. Each individual must be responsible for themselves. They must choose their own way and find their own truths. We must accept their way and they must accept our way, without judgements. Because to judge is not to let them be as they choose.

You can never force another person to see things your way. As individuals we all have our own perspectives and feel-ings. No two souls are the same, no two human beings are the same. We must learn to accept and know this to be true. You can only change your own perspective working on yourself. However, you can always share your understand-ing with others as you should do. Perhaps you can learn to see things from an other perspective. If quarrel arises be-cause of different opinions, you may consider that perhaps both are correct because they are different.

We should realize that there are no superior race or people, no superior knowledge, no superior religion, no superior country or world, that we all are here for the same reason to experience and learn in the physical world all we can, so that we may begin to learn in other dimensions what we cannot comprehend here; when we learn to accept another's right to his or her individual feelings, emotions and veins, then you can begin to have a mere balanced emotional self.

It is important to recognize the different emotions – anger, fear, joy, aggression, pain. They all are important. You must be able to have them all and accept them, not become too involved so that you as soul do not have control. You can always become overindulgent – that is not balanced – but only you as a person know your own individual limits, you are the only one who can control them. You must find your own balance.

Some people overeat, overdrink, oversmoke – even indulge too much or become addicted to anything like for example sex. Persons even become addicted to each other or situations out of habit, not wanting it so much but using it to compensate for some emotional lack or need. This is a danger and we must learn about our emotions and understand them to be able to see if we are using something or overdoing out of emotional attachment. It is important to be able to see our faults.

So sit down and ask yourself a few questions about your behavior: Do you react emotionally out of habit or do you really feel that way? Have you become overindulgent? Can you recognize when you have no emotional control?

Answer these questions on a separate paper. Also write down what your definition of love is. Write down all you can about all your feelings. Do you do things that you really enjoy or what others expect of you? Look in the mirror and ask: Who am I? Am I someone whom I know or someone that has been created by other's ideas of me? Do not let other people control your life. Set your own standards, do not try to compete or be other than what you are and what you want. You have the right to feel and act the way that really makes your life easier and to be happy. You will feel much better when you recognize and accept all your feelings as a part of you!

Emotional Evaluation Test

I. Below list six things that you think you should do, beginning with "I should ..."

Example: I should be more intelligent.

1. I should ...
2.
3.
4.
5.
6.

II. Now read each statement and ask yourself after each one, why you think you should do this or be that way.

Below write the answers:

1. I should be more intelligent because ...
2.
3.
4.
5.

You will be surprised that most answers apply to something other than because you want to.

III. Now reread the six "I should" statements in list I. Change the "I should" to "If I really wanted I could ..."

Example: If I really wanted, I could be more intelligent.

1. If I really wanted, I could ...
2.
3.
4.
5.

IV. Now reread list III. Then ask yourself "Why have I not?" after each statement. Write the answers below:

Example: I have not been more intelligent because ...

1. I have not been more ..., because ...
2.
3.
4.
5.

Now you have the answers to why you think you should do things, to why you have not and know that you can if you really want to.

V. Now on to the subject love or self-love:

I can feel love for ...

1. the very process of life itself
2. the joy of being alive
3. the beauty I see
4. another person
5. knowledge
6. the universe the way it is

What can you add to the list?

1.
2.
3.
4.
5.
6.

VI. Let us look at the ways you do not love yourself:

1. I scold and criticize myself endlessly.
2. I mistreat myself with food, alcohol or drugs.
3. I choose to believe I am unlovable.
4. I am not aware of my self-worth.
5. I create illness and pain in my body.
6. I procrastinate on things I can benefit from.
7. I live in chaos and disorder.
8. I create debts and burdens.
9. I attract lovers and mates that belittle me.

What can you add to the list?

1.
2.
3.
4.
5.
6.

VII. Lack of self-worth

1. In my marriage or relationship I am sure I am a failure.
2. I am afraid to ask for a raise or ask for more for my services.
3. My body does not match those in "Vogue magazine" or "Gentlemens's Quarterly".
4. If I do not make a sale or get the job I want I am sure "I am not good enough."
5. I am afraid of intimacy or allowing anyone too close. So I have anonymous sex.
6. I cannot make decisions because I am sure "it will be wrong or I will fail."

List some more ways you express your self lack.

1.
2.
3.
4.
5.

Learn to be like a baby. They can express themselves without being self-conscious – even loudly –, either anger or joy. Both are a part of life. The baby loves every part of its body and the processes. They do not worry if they will be loved or how they look. They only love and are loved. For what you send out – returns!

Chapter 3 – What Effect the Causal has

$\mathcal{T}$he causal dimension does indirectly and directly effect our lives. This is where all the records of your past incarnations are kept. Those who are spiritually adept and advanced have access to these records which are also referred to as Akashic records. Each soul can reach this level. Many individuals and spiritual groups actually do past life therapy and readings. These are often referred to as Akashic readings. Also many have experienced past life regressions on sessions. Sometimes these are helpful to learn about one's experiences and relationships within this lifetime by learning about one's past experiences. They also give a clear picture of one's relationships and experiences that are taking place now, to determine if it is a karmic or an unneeded experience that one has created.

You as an individual do create and choose your own life and experiences even if you do not consciously remember. Nothing happens by chance. Each soul before incarnation chooses the life they are to live based on past connections to other souls and particular experiences one needs to advance.

All these past choices, lives and experiences are stored in the causal bodies on the causal dimension which is a part of all souls. Sometimes the psychologists refer to it as the subconscious mind.

If a soul chooses a life experience but does not learn from the experience and does not advance, then unnecessary repetition occurs. Unfortunately, this takes place much too often – due to the limited teachings in societies here. If you do not know yourself to be a soul and are not aware of the other dimensions, you do not know that you choose this experience, which makes it more difficult to learn. Because you spend a great deal of time struggling, feeling confused, not understanding why you are here.

Once you learn to accept that you chose to be here, once you stop struggling against the experiences and see them as something for your own advancement then you are on your way – no longer stuck in the experiences. When you lack understanding, you become emotionally involved and mentally stressed – usually resulting in creating even more karmic debts for yourself! The statement that an experience that does not kill you will make you stronger is correct!

Learning to accept each experience as an opportunity for learning is a great step in making life easier to understand. Also to be able to examine the situation and to ask one-self questions about what was learned also helps to make the picture clear.

There are many keys to oneself recorded on the causal plane. Every soul has the ability to read their own past. I encourage this greatly, for all of one's past lives have much to do with what one is now and where one is now!

Now as a soul you have the ability to visit all of the dimensions of that I talk here. The soul has no limit except that which it creates itself. The soul can at will leave the physical and travel to any destination. You have a body for the soul to exist in on each dimension. That body corresponds to that particular dimension's vibrations for the protection of the soul, so that the soul can and does have a vehicle for each plane of dimension.

In chapter 10 I have laid out for you these dimensions and their correlating mantras. These mantras change the vibration of the soul and allow to experience and travel to the dimension they represent. One must of course ask for one's own spiritual protector to keep the physical body free of unwanted entities. Also tell your conscious mind that you will remember all you see, hear and experience. Sometimes the mind refuses to accept that which has not been programmed or is accepted as logical or believed in the physical realm! To reconnect the causal self with the conscious thinking mind one must insist that one will remember. Why? Because the mind is a tool for creating and recording. The soul is in charge. Too many believe that the mind is what is in control. What a mistake! But that is because the ones who whish to control want most to believe this. However, once we start to learn the truth, we are in control, not controlled! Then we no longer believe what others tell us. We know better. You must know, not believe. To believe something is subject to change. To know is unchangeable.

If you practice meditation regularly you begin to become adept in soul travelling. If you demand for the mind to remember an experience you reconnect the causal to the mind. You also put the soul in full control as it should be, for you are soul.

You need to understand all of your experiences, past and present, in order to be complete. One must accept all that one has done and been as a part of what one is. Every experience, whether it be divided into negative or positive, are valuable experiences that the soul needs for perfection here in the physical. The soul can then advance to learn in the other dimensions beyond this physical that which this body and brain cannot comprehend.

If we reconnect all the selves within this body – the physical, emotional, mental, causal and the etheric self – and see that all these experiences and all these selves are part of the soul's experience then we can begin to see how vast our universes are, how great we all are and how wonderful it is to be connected with all things created and be a part of that which created all! So accept the causal as an important part of all souls, for it has the key to that which we were and that which we are. Then we can really know our true selves as soul.

Chapter 4 – The Mental Process

$\mathcal{T}$ he mental process is a process for recording and remembering based on what you learn as a part of functioning in this particular existence. While the astral plane is based on emotions is thinking the base of the mental.

The mind and brain are much like a computer which must be programmed or fed with information – usually language, mathematics and logic. Most information is based on what concepts are physically accepted as reality. Many scientists, doctors and teachers focus on the mental process of learning. If a person becomes too mental then anything that is not logical is rejected. Therefore, we must understand and use the mental process but not become so caught up in it that we do not allow ourselves to understand concepts beyond the physical existence.

Most great scientists and inventors of the past were visionaries. They allowed for the possibility of realities beyond logic or accepted concepts. They were great thinkers but also had learned to work from higher levels such as intuition and gained great perspectives of so-called reality.

Einstein was such a man. He allowed himself to overcome the logic of accepted reality and go beyond to think that perhaps there was existence beyond the physical understanding. He realized that time is a man-made concept.

Nikola Tesla went beyond the accepted concepts of energy and found new sources of energy yet to be discovered or understood by most scientists of today.

Unfortunately, most people only learn within their limited borders of reality and have to repeat many lessons as they are not really thinking as an individual. They go through their lives accepting what they were taught and do not believe anything else, much like robots. Repeating the programs that were given them they learn from the teachers, parents, churches, culture, and the leaders of their societies. They accept that they are white, black, yellow, red – protestant, catholic, Jewish etc, or they are European, American, Asian. Then they are socialists, democratic, republican or left wing never asking if they really believe this, only repeating what they hear and consider it to be their own viewpoint. Even to be prejudiced is also learned.

The mental or thinking process was to be used as a tool for learning and creating. However, it has been manipulated by our societies here as a means of controlling people, not allowing them to think for themselves but being programed to fit into the scheme of designs and organizations of those who control. They are successful because most people fall into the trap. The trap being that you have no choice but to believe or be a certain way in order to fit in and be accepted by those around you. You believe you are victims of circumstances and need these agencies of control to exist here. In a way perhaps it is true – due to the fact that you contribute and support this world by thinking the way those who control want you to think!

How can you overcome it? It is really simple. Ask yourself questions about what you really believe. Do you indeed think that certain souls inhabiting a certain colored body makes them inferior? Do their religious beliefs really make them good or bad? If they are also the result of their society's programming are they not also victims? You are only a victim if you accept their truths as your own. Do not be a creature of habit going through life like a robot repeating the programmed messages like an answering machine. Wake up. Take a stand for yourself. Change your perspective. Allow yourself to really think about what you believe. The difference between you of Earth and us of Venus is that we do not believe something to be true. We know it to be so.

What is reality? Reality is only the perspective or view of someone or something. In order to understand you must be able to change your point of view, to accept that each individual has their own view or perspective of reality.

Example: You can look at a chair and it is small enough to sit on it for us human beings. To an insect it is very large and it can take much time to travel from the leg to the seat! It feels solid to us, however, to a photon it is only a collection of atoms and the photon can pass through! To us it looks stationary or still. But if you are in a spaceship in space the chair is spinning with the planet! To people in other countries they cannot see the chair! Yet it exists in your reality. So your perspective of the chair is relative to your point of view only. That is your reality, but not the only reality!

So we must learn to accept other views of reality and allow ourselves to think in terms that do not seem logical. We must not challenge other's concepts of reality but accept it as their view of reality. We all can only experience our own point of view. Each individual has the right to their own view or experience. Now you can see how we can learn to change our perspective or view.

Next we must learn how to overcome the limitations of what we think we have learned! Learning is a never ending process. Even when this temporary existence of life cycle is finished you still learn on other levels that are beyond your limited human concepts.

Remember there is no superior person, culture, religion, only choices that we make. However, you are taught that one religion, race or country is better than another. These are mental concepts and do not exist in reality. When I see or meet someone I do not see a black Christian or a white Catholic and so on. I see a soul inhabiting a physical body. Many are caught up in concepts of themselves. We are all in the learning process and much of how you think are other people's concepts, not your own. However, many of you have accepted these concepts as your own.

Also remember that if you believe and accept these concepts and believe that there is such a thing as superiority then you create much tension and conflicts in your life. Because to be superior one must find fault with others that they consider less superior. Therefore, conflicts arise and disagreements over beliefs. However, when you see things from a soul's level you know that these are false concepts, not truth. The truth is that whatever an individual chooses to study or satisfies their needs is good for them and they have the right to choose for themselves, just as you do.

There are many teachings available on earth, because there exist so many levels of consciousness. One can only find what they can relate to or understand according to their individual consciousness! Therefore, it is correct for them. However, you can change your consciousness and then you will find that you are no longer satisfied with many things you learned. That is advancement!

When you expand your consciousness. then you begin to seek answers to new questions. However, many never advance, they only believe whatever they were told and continue their life stuck in the program that was given them – by parents, teachers and society.

As you are now experiencing it is possible to change the thinking process. If you wish to be all that you were created to be then you must be willing to change and grow! Realize if you can that whatever you think or imagine is reality. If not yet in the physical it already exists on one of the higher dimensions. We are now experiencing realities that your greatgrandparents could not conceive of – such as computers, cable TV, satellites, space travel. At one time these were only existing possibilities. However, someone knew that it could exist and because they thought and imagined these concepts they became reality.

So the power to change your world lies in each individual, it only needs the desire to make it happen. So the future lies in yourself and the ability to create this by your thoughts. Remember wherever your attention goes the energy flows. So if you focus attention on negative issues you reinforce it with your energy. So you must make an effort to consciously focus your energy and thoughts on what you desire. Most people have been programmed to unconsciously focus on the negative. That is why earth has so many troubles within its societies. You must change the thinking process and reprogram yourself to use your energy in a constructive and positive way.

We have many abilities that lie dormant because they are never stimulated or used. Mental telepathy is possible for all, except that in your societies they are not considered common but rare gifts; most people believe that only a few possess such powers. In reality there are many abilities that you are created with but they cannot be used until you know it to be so.

Now the question is: How can I stop believing and learn to know? I am including at the end of this chapter a program to replace all the misinformation. However, remember it takes an effort of will. No matter how much important information you receive it is useless unless it is applied to your life daily. So the choice is yours.

Continue to be a robot or be a real individual able to think and create your own reality. Good luck!

How-to-just-be-Program

I am in the present – the now.

All is perfect, whole and balanced.

I do not believe in old limitations and lacks.

I do not judge but accept and understand.

I am as I was created to be perfect and whole. Free of the past it has no control only to learn from it.

I open myself to the wisdom that is part of that which created me and is part of me and within me.

I move on to the new, forward to release old patterns.

The more resentment I release, the more I can receive and give love.

I love all as I wish to be loved.

I see myself as an individual – unique and special.

All my experiences have formed the facets of the special jewel like no other which is myself.

I see myself as soul and this body only as a vehicle for this world. For I am part of the Creator and the energy that I come from.

Every day I am what I choose and think thoughts that create what I choose.

I allow all to be what they choose.

I am balanced in all I do.

I am not a victim of circumstances or other's standards but the master of my destiny.

I am whole.

I achieve the greatness that I am.

Chapter 5 – The Function of the Etheric Body

*T*he etheric is the first dimension the soul crosses when leaving the pure spiritual planes. It is the division between the non-material or pure energy and the material dimensions. It is the first body the soul has for protection in the lower material worlds, planes or dimensions. It is also the dimension that controls our concepts of faith in the supreme being as God. It directly is responsible for our ability to know ourselves as soul and to allow us to understand our divine connection to the Creator.

All saints, spiritual leaders and masters draw their energy from the etheric. It is each soul's direct contact to spirituality. It allows us to know and believe in God. It is an essential and necessary link to our spiritual development. It is from there that we have the surge of faith and ultimate power to believe and eventually know of the power of God, to be able to feel it and use it to convince others. It is the connection of the soul to the higher Godworlds! For here it is where all spiritual energy flows from the place where the soul and all that is began. It is our divine link to the Creator. All miracles, the power of prayer, healing and the will to be great begins. This is the dimension that we strive to reach ultimately before we are spiritually complete in these lower worlds as we journey back to that which we came from!

We journey from that which created us, not aware that we are to experience ultimately through thousands of incarnations, that we are a part of that which created us, but with the knowledge that we are, and an understanding of that which created all and the aim to become a part of it and become creators ourselves.

Much of this knowledge is forgotten as we reincarnate into new bodies with new minds and spend much time adapting to and learning to use our new bodies and understand our ever new experiences.

So therefore much is stored away in the subconscious selves which operate and experience much in the non-material worlds as soul whereas our conscious mind knows very little of this great knowledge, ever seeking that which is already in us. Few souls reincarnate with all knowledge and experiences intact, not separated but whole and fully aware of all. These are the ones who no longer have to return into the physical but choose to come and share all with those who open themselves and desire to know, bringing with them the truth of our creation. Of course, there are those who laugh and ridicule these individuals and it is a struggle to overcome these difficulties. It takes perseverance and strength for there is a constant battle between the negative powers which rule the lower worlds and those who bring truth and light.

However, inside most is the deep feeling that they know what we bring to be true. This is the etheric self trying to reconnect all the experiences of the true self to the physical self that resides here!

Many great spiritual beings have come and gone and will continue to do so until all souls are enlightened and the earth eventually changes to the divine place it should be – with all beings here understanding and accepting each other as soul and disregarding the division created by the controlling factors here, just as time is a man-made concept to divide one's days and years here. In reality it does not exist. Your time here in one's life is equal to a grain of sand for the soul is eternal and shall always be.

So it is vital that you reconnect to the etheric and overcome the so-called subconscious self and connect all within you so that there is no division.

Chapter 6 – The Soul, the real I

*I*n the past chapters I have been driving home this point of understanding yourself as a soul.

For those who do not understand our concepts of the creation of the soul I have a simple concept which I will disclose to you. I have tried to help you understand all the parts of yourself that you know of – the physical, emotional, mental, causal, etheric, and now the soul, the real you. All these are necessary parts of a human being to help you function. The soul is the essence, the part that remains in control and intact always, life after life. Even though you have a connection to all living entities you were created as an individual and shall always be so, because each soul has its own individual experiences that will not even be the same as the ones of another!

When we learn to change our perspective and view life and experiences and others as soul, from a soul point of view, we have the great ability to view things as a whole, not separated, not from the emotional, mental or personal life situation, but with a greater understanding of ourselves and a greater acceptance and understanding of other souls as unique individuals, without judgement or resentment but acceptance and love – as it was meant to be.

The concept of creation is as follows:

Take a centrifuge which is used to spin material at a fast rate or speed. Then you put into this centrifuge rocks, sand and water, and you will see that the materials begin to separate. The rocks which are a heavier material will fly to the outer edge of the centrifuge, and as you look toward the center you see less and less material - the sand, then water and in the midst only air.

This is like the dimensions. The material of our physical world could be compared to the rocks – lying on the outmost edge, and each lighter material representing the dimen-sions above the physical or beyond the physical. The center part, the air, represents the pure spiritual or non-material dimension. This could be compared to the God planes or the place of creation!

All energy spins in a spiral like formation, even galaxies. This is the secret of creation, for all energy forms a vortex around all living things creating its own magnetic field. So every living thing is not unlike a planet as it has its own vortex of energy.

The Creator is not a being but a great intelligent mass of the most powerful energy and with unimaginable knowledge. To be sure that it would never cease to exist it procreated from itself all the universes, galaxies, life forms and souls to continue in a never ending cycle of evolution and recreation.

We as souls are part of this plan to build, grow, and continue to gain knowledge, power and be omnipowerful and omnipresent always without end, and there is no end to the creation or evolution of souls. We are and always shall be flowing like a spiral from what we were created, to learn, grow, become powerful and eventually return and become a part once again of the power that created us, only with knowledge and experience that we lacked in the beginning of our journey. So we shall always be a part of that which created us and that is why we must eventually learn to create what we wish – be it for the good of all, that we are a part of.

When the soul was first created it was only pure energy, light, that did not know it ex-isted. So it began its journey from the center of the creation down - across the etheric, the causal, the mental, the astral, and the first stop, the physical.

Remember: The etheric allows the soul to remember and feel its spiritual connection, the causal to store its experiences on all dimensions, the mental to be able to think, record and communicate, the astral to feel, then the physical to experience all these functions in order to learn from each life incarnation.

So the soul is sheathed and protected on its journey by a corresponding body from each of the before mentioned dimensions. How wonderful and great it is to be!

When the soul first came to the physical it was not in the human form, oh no, sorry to disappoint you. There is an evolutionary cycle that must be followed as all living things do. Even planets as you may have read in my book "From Venus I Came" go through cycles of evolution!

So when the soul first arrived in the physical on whatever planet in whatever system it first went into the state of being and experiencing as a mineral, yes mineral, the mineral state of existence. The soul has to be every mineral on every planet in every solar system and serve a purpose in every existence before it can advance. What? I can hear the gasps. What a blow to the ego to be a lowly mineral! Well, the soul must be everything in order to understand everything!

Experience is the only true teacher. So use your imagination. What experiences can a mineral have? What purposes can a mineral have? Well, there are minerals in water, for plants, for animals, for humans. What about rocks for homes, tools, jewels? Wow, there are many possibilities we overlook being the great humans we now are! So a soul spends some thousands of years incarnating over and over in different mineral states waiting for the opportunity to serve a purpose, for its existence has to mean something. I know on one hand it is frightening, on the other amusing. Actually it is quiet beneficial.

Finally after you as soul have exhausted all the possiblities of being a mineral you graduate and advance to the plant stage. Now you go through the same procedure being all the plants, serving all the possible or imaginable purposes on every planet, everywhere. Is it not delightful, to find out how vast our history really is!

Just as before when you have no more plant options left you get to incarnate as an animal! How delightful! Of course you get to be wild, domestic, serve as food or musicances or beauty. But you must be all – fowl, fish, bird and mamals, just as before everywhere within all the known and unknown universes or galaxies.

Finally after this you get to become the wonderful human being – or sometimes not so wonderful. For as before you must be all that human beings can be, all races, sexes, mentalities or lack of. That means being evil, a murderer, retarded, a genius, a musical-artist and so on; you name it, this you have been or will be. Are you exhausted by the idea yet?

Well, do not be discouraged. By now most of you have most of this been in the past, otherwise you would not be evolved enough to read this or be interested. Does that make you feel better? I hope so, for no matter what you have experienced or been, you are still a soul.

Between all these mind-reeling lifetimes, and before the soul is reincarnated in any new cycle of its chosen destiny, the soul has a period of rest on a special part of the astral realm where it is tended to by older souls who have chosen this as their own particular mission after their physical incarnations are complete. These angelic like beings care for and help the soul choose and adjust to their new life to be. It is like a nursery for souls, where the soul recovers from the previous life cycle and prepares for the next. It is a place of recuperation and regeneration through love and devotion of these special caretakers.

I have come to make it already here and now easier for you, for the more you learn now the less you have to go through!

Now as you have learned being a human being is more complicated because you form families and sometimes relationships – be it personal or within work – that you may or may not want. However, you cannot blame anyone for you have free will and choices, unfortunately many are made because of confusion or a feeling you have to, most are made because you have not been properly informed or you have been misinformed, unfortunately.

That is exactly why I wrote this book to help you. If your head is reeling by now, take a break, meditate, have a cigarette, a drink, a walk or whatever you do to relax. It is hard for the small part of the human brain on earth, that you have been allowed, to assimilate such information. Actually I have been taught to use much more of the brain than you and I need.

It might be hard for you if you just picked up this book out of curiosity without reading any of my other texts or attending one of my workshops. However, I really am trying to make it simple and understandable. Much of what I am writing has been through experience of my life here these last 40 years and part of what I was taught prior to living on earth.

Now you have an idea of what it is like to be a soul as we all are. It is very important to never forget, to remember this just till the end of your life here. This gives you the opportunity to advance faster. I hope it also helps you to understand yourselves on all levels as it was meant to do, so that you can have a greater perspective and help create with your own presence and power the world as it should be – with room and acceptance for all souls in all forms. Seeing as how we have all been these different life forms should we not have greater compassion and love for all things that are?! Should we not love and accept every soul and respect them for their individual struggles to exist? Should we not try to help those confused by the information they receive? Is it not our duty as ones who know more, to share and help those who are wandering around, committing terrible injustices toward others? You must understand that with knowledge comes responsibility for how we continue to be! For if we know better, we shall be better. There is no good nor evil, only ignorance.

However, it is not to be used to be superior but to enlighten and be always thankful to our Creator for allowing us to know what is true and right. That is being soul, the real you!

Chapter 7 – About Karma

*K*arma is perhaps often misunderstood. Many regard karma as a punishment for past or present deeds.

In reality karma can be positive or difficult experiences. Karma also can be rewards for positive deeds or actions. All depends on the soul – the awareness, the experiences and the responsibilities of each particular soul.

The more aware one is and the more responsible one becomes toward one's own actions and relations, has a lot to do as to the amount of karma one accumulates whether it be negative or positive. This is why I keep repeating throughout this book and in my encounters with individuals the importance of recognizing one's own part in misunderstandings and involvement with family, loved ones and mere acquaintances. The more we keep our relationships clear, harmonious and balanced, the less we have attachments and ties with other souls. This eliminates unnecessary karma or lessons. The more we take care now, the faster we can progress, because we then do not need to repeat experiences we have not yet learned or taken on responsibility.

Basic karma is accumulated not only in the physical but on the other dimensions as well. This is necessary for each soul's development and interaction with other souls. So basic karma is carried with us to help achieve and learn.

Unnecessary karma is unlike basic karma. It is created in

past and present life situations through attachments to emotional situations and the lack of understanding of the importance of our part in clearing these up before we end that particular life cycle. Any unfinished business does not cease with the existence of our particular body in any life cycle. It must be cleared either through reincarnation in the physical – with whom ever – or on another dimension as you encounter the soul or souls with whom you still have something to clear.

Then there is good karma that which one reaps in turn for selfless caring for others and for good deeds. Good karma can be through sacrifice whether it be emotional, mental, physical and so on. But it must not be done so as to get a reward but as a true unselfish act. If one's life cycle ends, then the good karma can be awarded or experienced on other dimensions or in a future physical incarnation.

The difficult part is to always to take care to keep one's relationships balanced and free of traumatic unsolved situations, and not to become too egoistical or attached to people, material wealth, or to feel superior in any way. For all experiences are for our benefit and learning – not to belittle others or control.

In reality from a soul's point of view the negative and positive does not exist. All experiences are relative and important for the balancing and perfection of the soul. I have used the examples of basic karma – negative and good – to help you understand that karma is not a punishment but more of a result of your individual life choices and involvement with others souls on your journey from creation into your physical existences. It is also effective in the other dimensions, in case you no longer have to be part of the physical. However, all depends on you – on your choices and how much you learn, accomplish, and – most of all – the responsibility that you accept in these life cycles and experiences.

So karma is only the result of cause and effect. You always want to be the cause, not the effect.

Laws of the Supreme Deity

There are seven basic laws and seven divine laws of the Supreme Deity.

The seven basic laws are:

1. Know ourselves to be part of the Creator.
2. Be thankful for the experience of existing.
3. Not judge but accept all beings.
4. To know we have existed as all living forms.
5. Fulfill our responsibilities in each life cycle.
6. Obey laws of nature and societies in which we exist.
7. Learn from mistakes so as not to repeat old lessons.

The seven divine laws are:

1. Love all living creations.
2. Use our energy to support our worlds.
3. Share knowledge and wisdom.
4. Understand the equality of all souls.
5. Never use power to manipulate or control.
6. Know that the soul is immortal.
7. Give thanks to the One Divine Being daily.

These laws have existed since creation began. If one knows, remembers and lives according to the laws of the Supreme Deity, it is possible to overcome much karma and have a vast overview of oneself in relation to all existence. Unlike man-made rules these do not apply to only limited teachings or societies, but encompass all life existences, and they do not interfere with any social or religious beliefs.

These laws allow for individual choices and freedom wherever the soul is at any time. The soul can still abide by the teachings or laws of chosen spiritual paths or societies.

These laws also help one to advance with acceptance instead of judgement of other living entities – to better understand them from a soul's point of existence as the Supreme Creator intends and allows us to exist!

Chapter 8 – Meditation

editation is now categorized with esoteric and new age concepts. The opposite is true. It is very ancient and universally known. It is one of the oldest practices and yet had to be reintroduced because of dominating religious organization's condemnation of its use in the past. It was associated with pagan teachings or occult uses. In reality it was used to focus on the inner self and to view the other dimensions not related to the physical.

Meditation is a way to tune into that energy source that gives the life force to all that is, to become aware of it and become a part of it, to be able to direct and control the forces that already exist within and about oneself.

We are not victims of circumstances as the ones who wish to control us wish us to believe. We have a choice to be the creators of our destinies. As soul we have free will over every experience and everything we encounter in our journey through our many incarnations. So do not be a victim of circumstances, but master of your destiny!

Meditation Techniques

There are many meditation procedures. Being unique and individual you must experience and find one that is beneficial and works for you.

The Sufis spiral around spinning rapidly until the physical body collapses and the soul is believed to be sent spiraling away! There is the yogi who has a special cross-legged sitting position. You may lie on your back or sit comfortably in a chair.

I believe it is important to be as comfortable as possible, so that you do not experience a cramp or an uncomfortable part of your body. The back should be straight but not stiff. The hands should touch or fingers clasped, thumbs touching. Feet should also be touching or if lying down cross the legs. This creates a channel through which the energy flow is directed. It flows from the crown chakra down to the feet and then around the body through the hands. By all these parts touching the energy can create a vortex all around the physical self. Of course you can concentrate on one specific chakra if desired.

You should focus the attention on the area just above and between the eyes – as if there were a viewing screen there. Focus with the mind, not with the physical eyes.

You should always take three deep cleansing breaths to relief tension and rid the body of negative energy.

Soft music is helpful to play and focus on after you repeat your selected mantra. There are many tapes for meditation available.

Always choose ten to thirty minutes that can be uninterrupted and quiet. Earplugs are also helpful. You can meditate anytime that you choose or even while lying in bed as preparing to sleep. If you fall asleep it is alright as most of us learn on the other dimensions while in a dream state.

Experiences

Experiences are subtle and you have to condition the senses to respond and the subconscious mind has to be programmed. To rely the experiences to the physical, mental and emotional experiences you must repeat to yourself that you wish to remember what you experience, see or hear. Also always ask for your spiritual protector or guide to ensure that you are safe from unwanted disembodied entities.

Notice any lights, patterns, sounds or change in feelings. Do not have expectations, just learn to experience and accept. Relax and enjoy. Remember do not compare your experience to someone else's experience. You are an individual and must have your own experience. Be adventurous and try different techniques. You may create your own way!

Some people find looking at nature a source of inspiration and a kind of meditation. Others find dancing is a way. You must learn about yourself and what really inspires you. Meditation means focusing the attention in one direction and absorbing all you can physically, emotionally, mentally and spiritually from what ever you focus on or choose as a focus point for your meditation. You can even just star at a star, a candle, a crystal, a stream, the sky – even another person. So just learn to be, to be free to experience what you can.

Creative Exercise

For this exercise it is beneficial to darken the room. Lie in the bed or sit in meditation position. Take three deep breaths, relax. It must be very quiet, earplugs also work. So you have no outside influences. First visualize this earth, all its inhabitants, the oceans, forests, fields, cities. Picture yourself as part of it. Feel the life and activity all around you – voices, traffic, noise.

Now eliminate all the buildings and manmade structures. See only nature and living things. Focus on this for a moment. Then remove all moving living creatures – except yourself. See how still and quiet all is. Even the wind ceases to blow. Listen to the silence. Now remove all things on the surface of the earth. Now you see only a ball – no color, no life, no movement. Hanging in space you are still present, viewing it. Now take away the planet, leave only yourself. You are in space – with nothing around you. Feel the strangeness of being the only thing existing with nothingness all around you.

Now try to visualize that you disappear and you do not exist. Now there is nothingness. This should give you a very eerie feeling. It is also very difficult to visualize nothing. You should now return and feel the relief of being part of all creation that exists and that you helped to create.

Chapter 9 – Soul Travel Technique

hile the so-called astral projection limits the experience to the astral dimension, soul travel allows temporarily the departure of the soul from the physical existence. Astral projection means to leave the physical body in the astral body which is attached to the physical by the silver chord. Unlike this the soul travel technique enables you to leave the physical body without the connection of the silver chord. You travel with light and sound and have access to any dimension you wish, where you can gain knowledge or make an experience for the benefit of the soul while still existing in the physical.

In the next chapter I have made available to you mantras for each existing dimension including the physical realm. Each dimension actually has many divisions that would take many years of exploring to understand and recognize and of which I could write a whole book. Paul Twitchell, the founder of Eckankar, has described them within numerous individual lessons for students. His books are available, also in German.

I have condensed the different levels for simplicity to fit our busy lifestyles without losing the essence. For thousands of years these were secret teachings taught by many chosen spiritual masters from many worlds and many cultures. They are ancient – older than earth. They were brought here and placed under protection by ancient masters of the spiritual hierarchy so that they always would exist and not fall into the control of ones who manipulate or wish to keep them for selfish reasons from the common people.

In the early 1940s and 50s the plans were laid to make these teachings available to the masses, as it was known that people's consciousness was changing and the New Age was nearing. This is now also part of my mission along with many other teachers today, so that truth can prevail over the negative powers that control the souls with fear as a tool for manipulation. At least each soul has available the choice once again!

The first step is of course to recognize that you are soul, not the physical body or mentality. The second step is knowing of the different dimensions and the mantras for each one. The third step is to practice daily the meditation procedures. But above all is the desire to experience without fear!

Of course, you must choose a time when you will not be disturbed by physical noise or interference for at least thirty minutes or longer. Close your eyes and bring yourself in a comfortable position – sitting straight on a chair or on the floor or lying relaxed in bed. You must clear the mind of thoughts and concentrate on the inner self. Be aware of the heart beat and breath slowly and rhythmically. Relax the whole physical body, free yourself of tensions – be it mental, emotional or physical.

See yourself bundling up all these tensions and discarding them in the ocean of light. They will return if it is to be.

It is better if you are in a dim lighted or darkened room so that the images within are not interfered with. You must decide where you wish to travel and for what reason, then choose the mantra for that dimension (see next chapter).

Then repeat the mantra out loud six to nine times, breathe in and as you exhale chant the mantra as long as the breath allows, letting the sound encompass you.

Ask your spiritual guide for protection. Look for any point of blue white light. Also pay attention to any color or images, letting yourself be drawn into whatever you are visualizing. Be aware of any high pitched sound – a whistling or humming or any subtle noise taking place inside of one's ears. Be aware of any tingling or feeling. Sometimes one feels as if the top of the head or the third eye area opens. Follow any light or image. Focus on it and become it. It may be subtle at first but will intensify with daily practice.

If you return and remember anything, no matter how insignificant it may seem, write it down. If you feel as if you doze off and sleep in, this is quite normal. This happens when one is not ready to consciously accept the experience, but it will change as one gets used to it and practices. Eventually the subconscious will reconnect to the conscious mind and the connection will remain. It has to be reconnected out of use, much like an electrical appliance that has lain around and in which the connections have accumulated dust. It has to be burnt off to renew the circuit. So it is with the inner connections of each being! It improves with use – do not become discouraged. Perseverance and patience pay off!

The Hu mantra is good for beginners as it is powerful and encompasses all the dimensions. You may also practice before going to sleep. Good luck and good journeys!

Chapter 10 – Mantras and their Benefits

This is an introduction to the Venusian understanding of the different dimensions, their corresponding colors, sounds and the mantras that represent the vibrations of these dimensions, also to the benefits that they have on us living here in the physical. It is essential for practicing soul travel as I have described in the last chapter.

On the following pages are individual listings, features, directions and benefits for each dimension to help you in your daily life here. I have found them very helpful to me. I hope you enjoy and practice these!

Physical Dimension

Alaya is the mantra representing the physical dimension and is spiritually in harmony with the specific vibrations of the physical level. Pronounced "Ah-lah-ya" it should be repeated at least three times very slowly while visualizing the color green that symbolizes the physical. The predominating sound is thunder and drums. These represent the basic vibration of the physical.

When involved in physically strenuous activities this mantra is beneficial in creating the balance of energy and strength needed to reinforce the physical self.

Astral Dimension

Kala is the mantra representing the astral dimension. Chanted loudly it helps to make experiences on the astral dimension from this level. Pronounced "Kah-lah" it should be repeated at least four times very slowly while visualizing the color pink which is the color of the astral.

The sounds that predominate the astral are the sounds of the ocean. This mantra is beneficial for balancing and harmonizing the emotional body. When you are in very stressful emotional states or have difficulty controlling the emotions it affects everyone differently depending on one's feelings. It can make you cry or feel happy – both are beneficial in balancing your feelings.

Causal Dimension

Aum is the mantra for the causal plane on which the experiences of the souls are recorded. It is therefore beneficial to bring past life remembrances in one's subconscious mind to the surface. It is pronounced "A-oh-m" and should be repeated slowly at least five times. The color of the causal is purple and the sound is tingling bells.

Mental Dimension

Mana is the mantra for the mental plane. It is pronounced "Mah-nah". It should be repeated at least six times slowly while visualizing its representing color of blue. The sound is flowing or trickling water. This mantra is beneficial for stimulating the thinking process for those who use computers, do typing or are teaching science. It balances and harmonizes the thinking process. It can eliminate confusion and stress related to the mental process.

Etheric Dimension

Baju is the mantra for the etheric plane. This is the first shell or body that the soul takes on when after it is created it starts its downward spiraling journey to the lower dimensions and their divisions – the negative and positive planes or dimensions. This is beneficial for inspiring or creative work. It is the closest to the soul. It is pronounced "Bah-ju". It should be repeated slowly seven times. The color gold should be visualized as it represents the etheric. The sound of this dimension is a humming sound or the sound of bees. It can be a deep humming. It stimulates the creative energy within oneself.

Soul Dimension

Shanti is the mantra for this dimension. It is pronounced "Shan-tee". It should be repeated slowly at least eight times. The color of the soul dimension is pale yellow. The sound is stark wind. This mantra is beneficial in harmonizing all the before mentioned bodies and creating a very peaceful feeling of contentment. Also it is beneficial in healing physical injuries, emotional crises, mental illness or depression or difficulty in any area of one's functions.

Anami Lok Dimension

Hu is the mantra for the dimension called the void of creation where all energy that created all there is and all souls flows from. It is the center of creation. It is pronounced "Ha-you". It should be repeated at least nine times. The corresponding color is white, the sound is music of the universe. It is beneficial for spiritual enlightenment, helps to raise the consciousness and changes the perspective view of an individual. It is where we began and shall seek to return to for all knowledge.

Each of these mantras raises the vibration of the soul to the level of the dimension it represents and allows a learning process to be experienced there.[1]

---

1 There is a Soul Journey Meditation available from Omnec as CD and download. Please see recommendations on the last pages of this book.

Dimension	Mantra	Sound	Color
Anami Lok (God Plane)	HU	Music of the universe *(cannot be described in words)*	White
Soul	SHAN-TI	Stark wind	Yellow
Etheric	BAJU	Humming of bees	Gold
Mental	MANA	Flowing of water	Blue
Causal	AUM (OM)	Ringing of little bells	Purple or violet
Astral	KALA	Ocean breeze	Rose/Pink
Physical	ALAYA	Thunderstorm	Green

Anami Lok - God Planes
Mantra: HU
Sound: Sound of the Universe
Ruler: SUGMAD

Soul Dimension Mantra: SHANTI
Sound: Stark Wind
Ruler: SAT NAM

Etheric Dimension   Mantra: BAJU
Sound: Humming
Ruler: SOHANG

Mental Dimension   Mantra: MANA
Sound: Flowing Water
Ruler: OMKAR

Causal Dimension   Mantra: AUM
Sound: Tingling Bells
Ruler: RAMKAR

Astral Dimension   Mantra: KALA
Sound: Sound of the Ocean
Ruler: JOT NIRANJAN

Physical Dimension   Mantra: ALAYA
Sound: Thunder and Drums
Ruler: ELAM

„The Godworlds" Illustration from © Anja Schäfer | www.venus-spirit.com | www.omnec-onec.com

Image 2: The Godworlds

Chapter 11 – Healing and Self-healing Procedures

*Y*ou must know that you as a divine being have the power to heal yourself. It is much better to heal oneself rather than trying to heal others. We should always love and comfort others, however, one must have permission to heal others and must be aware that sometimes a condition may be karmic or any learning experience for that particular soul. So precautions are to be taken before attempting to heal other individuals so as not to break any spiritual laws. Also one should be aware that they might take the illness upon themselves as it being a kind of energy that must be transferred elsewhere. Therefore, it is important to understand that we do not have the power to make such decisions. There are laws of the Supreme Deity that all the experiences one goes through have been chosen before this lifetime by each individual soul!

If you are concerned about someone that you care for who is ill, then you must follow the procedure listed below to insure that you are protected and that you are not taking away an experience that is necessary. Remember this life is transient and the soul is eternal and immortal. Usually the most painful and difficult experiences are the most valuable for learning.

If you wish to help others, then first you must discuss it with them to be sure it is not against their own particular beliefs. You do not want to interfere with one's own choices. Then you must tell them that if they are not healed it will be up to the highest power. If they are healed, it means that it was not a necessary experience and if they are not then there is a lesson in the experience.

It can be done in their presence or even from different locations. Time and distance do not affect such divine powers.

If done with the individual they may lie down with feet touching or crossed, eyes closed focusing on the third eye area with the mind as if there were a TV screen on the inside of their head. They should take three deep breaths and relax. You sit straight and relaxed in a chair nearby, feet touching, hands clasped. You take three deep breaths and also focus on the third eye area.

Now you visualize this person's face in a snowball. Then you visualize yourself taking this ball and throwing it into the ocean of love and mercy. It is a stream of blue-white energy made up of advanced souls and ascended masters' energy. It flows from the God center through all dimensions and universes. You picture the snow ball being absorbed into this stream, becoming part of it. Then you say:

"In the name of the Divine Creator, I ask that if it is to be that this illness be taken away. We accept your divine decision whatever it will be. I give thanks to all that is. Baraka Bashad."

Then you are finished. You may do the same procedure even thousands of miles apart as long as you have discussed it with the person before. You may do it at night while lying in bed just before sleep. Just let the person know when you will do it, so they can be relaxed and receptive at the time, also their ability to draw upon the energy themselves is important. It is always important that we understand that we may use this energy which is a part of us but that we are not really doing the healing. It is a combination of our knowing that it is possible and that we are directing the energy. But if the ego becomes involved and the individual takes the credit then it becomes dangerous because it is sort of a manipulation of the divine source of energy. We must always acknowledge the great source that generates the energy and be grateful for the ability to use and direct this energy but not say we are doing the healing.

To heal oneself one must follow the same procedure only visualizing the illness of oneself in the snowball. Lying down is very good as one is more relaxed and focussed.

Another procedure is to see the person's face and surround them with pure blue-white light energy and ask for protection for that person or oneself and always send love to the individual and see yourself surrounded and protected by the same light and energy. Try to feel the warm energy as it flows through and around you. The more you focus on this the stronger it becomes. However, one must know without a doubt it is so.

It is always good before any meditation or healing to call on your own particular spiritual guide or guardian to protect you from undesirable entities so that they may not attach themselves to you and use you for their desires. Such experiences have been witnessed and documented in the cases of so-called possessions by individuals. These are unfortunate incidents that occur when a person attempts to experiment with occult and psychic phenomenon without proper understanding or protection. It can be a very devastating if not destructive experience and can lead to an unnecessary end to one's otherwise planned life experience, causing one to have to reincarnate and go through certain lessons unnecessarily.

Many beings on their quest for spiritual enlightenment fall into traps of experimenting with such dangerous experiences. However, most of us have already gone through these ordeals and shun such things because of a deep fear from the past and know that it has already been experienced and do not have the ability or desire to encounter such things again. Once the soul has experienced or learned a certain lesson it avoids such experiences out of remembering and not feeling the desire to repeat them. Sometimes however, human beings fall into traps because of unawareness and not paying attention to their own feelings of precaution.

Always take the time to ask yourself *why* you want to heal someone or yourself, examine the reason to be sure it is out of love and the desire to help and not for the feeling that you need recognition or a sense of accomplishment. Remember to live in harmony and balance; to face the individual responsibility of your life is a very great accomplishment. To be aware of such energy and to use it the proper way without breaking spiritual laws or endangering yourself and others is important and also a great accomplishment. To love all and oneself as a part of the Creator and as the Creator created you out of love is a giant step on your path of existence.

Chapter 12 – Energy – Ways to feel and use it daily

*E*verything that exists is made of energy at different vibrations. In the material worlds energy moves slower and becomes more dense or solid. The higher you go beyond the physical the faster is the vibration of energy. That is why it is difficult to perceive these energies in the physical body. They are usually beyond the ability of our human eyes and ears. Only at times we may be sensitive to them as soul. Whenever you hear the high-pitched sounds in your ears or beeping, whining, it is the sound of the other dimensions entering through the chakras, and it is heard inside oneself. The connection is made by the correlating spiritual body that belongs to that certain dimension.

For instance, when a person meditates and repeats the mantra for a specific dimension and is focusing on the color and the sound that represent that dimension, they may hear the sound of the dimension through that body, whether it be the astral, causal, mental, etheric or soul plane.

Within your physical self there are all these other bodies that the soul picked up on its journey from the dimension in which it was created. As it crossed these planes or dimensions it picked up a protective shell or body for protection. Being pure energy the soul cannot exist in the lower dimensions without a correlating body that is made of the same energy as that dimension. So inside the physical are many other energy bodies.

The physical body is made up of the same energy as all things in the physical surroundings. So it is a vehicle and a protection for the other bodies and the soul. As the soul leaves the physical it also drops or leaves the physical body in the physical dimension, and as it journeys higher it leaves behind on each dimension the shell or body of that plane. It only picks up the bodies as it enters the dimension again when needed.

If you watch a propeller or fan blade before you turn on the motor which powers the movement, the blades look solid, but when their movement increases and they move faster they become unvisible. So as energy increases it hangs into another form of existence.

Now the energy that flows through and supports all life is the Creator or God as most here know it. We are all as soul part of this Creator and Its creation. We all have a divine beginning and purpose to our existence. We are sent to the physical to learn and experience all that a soul can. Part of the growth from not understanding or knowing we are soul is to know this and then become creators ourselves. To create your own destiny is what we do. We choose our life before we are born into the physical and then spend much time struggling against that which we must learn. When one learns to accept and goes through whatever happens, then you are on your way to learning at a faster rate and having a higher understanding of oneself and life.

Now to be able to feel the energy and direct it is simple. It only takes practice as does anything. You may sit with your back straight, feet together to create the best connection between you, the earth and its energy and to allow the energy from the cosmos to flow.

You always take three deep breaths to relax your muscles of tension. You do not close your eyes for this. You place the palms of your hands together in the prayer position about three inches from the body and in the center of the chest area. Hold them pressed tightly together until you feel warmth. You may also rub them together about seven times until they become warm. After you feel both hands become warm slowly separate the hands about four inches and bend the fingers toward one another. Focus your attention on your hands and become aware of a slight electric tingle between them that is jumping back and forth the fingertips. Now lower one hand slowly, then the other. You alternate each hand and raising and lowering you can feel the change in energy.

You may also try it with a friend. After you both have separated your hands and feel your own energy then turn toward one another keeping hands apart. Do not touch other fingers, there must be at least one to one and a half inches apart. Slowly pull hands far apart and feel the energy intensify as you bring them close again. Now this energy flows through and around us and if we have the chakras open it flows in more. Of course, awareness has a lot to do with it. It is there but goes unnoticed. The key to its use is to know and direct it with your thoughts. The more you use the energy the more powerful it becomes. Sometimes you may feel your hands become hot, then you know that there is a strong energy flowing.

When you meditate you are drawing energy in at will and it interferes as you repeat the mantras. Meditation is a kind of spiritual cleansing of all the bodies as the energy flows in the dissipated and polluted areas and used energy flows out to be regenerated.

Every living thing has its own energy field. When you are out in the nature try to build up the energy in your hands and hold them close to the trees, rocks and plants. See if you can feel the energy. Also if you take off your shoes you can be regenerated with the powerful energy of the earth itself.

Did you ever take a moon beam shower af full moon? It also generates its own special energy.

Energy can be seen by trained or sensitive people as auras. Have a friend sit in a chair by a blank white wall. Now stare at him indirectly without really focusing. Take in the wall around them as well and you will begin to see a faint outline of them. The more you practice the clearer it becomes and even color will appear!

It is important for you to try and put your attention on positive things and not reinforce negativity with your energy. Remember where your attention goes the energy flows. So do not put attention on what disturbs you or causes emotional stress. Focus on good and constructive experiences. If you worry about becoming ill or a war or anything you are reinforcing it and may cause it to happen. Always bless the war stricken places. Always know that good will prevail and do not foresee doom and negativeness. I know that if something irritates me and I pay attention to it, it seems to become worse, but if I just put my attention elsewhere it does not bother me. So you just take your attention and energy away. Therefore you are using your energy in a constructive and positive way. Then you are doing your part to create a better world for you and others! On the following pages are some mantras that will help you increase your energy.

Power Punch for every day

You must stand with your face to the light of a window. You close your eyes and take a deep breath in. You exhale as if forcing all negative energy out of yourself.

Then you take another deep breath, and as you inhale you visualize light energy being sucked in through all chakras and especially the crown chakra.

You feel the power of energy. That is your life force that connects you with all living things created by the one infinite power source. It is unlimited. So absorb as much as you want, you must see it flowing in and around you.

In the center of your body, the solar plexus, visualize a red alert button. Imagine it being activated by this energy. It starts to glow and soon you are glowing, now filled with energy.

Operation Push is in action! Now you can accomplish all you desire and be a supreme example to everyone around you.

Now open your eyes, give thanks to life and all it can offer and be a powerful force of the One.

Song Mantra

May the long time sunshine find me,

all love surround me.

May the pure light within me

find its way out!

(This can be done anywhere.)

Sweet Dreams Vision

As you prepare for sleep and close your eyes you say to yourself:

"I am surrounded by the light, I am protected by the light, and I walk in the light. God is the light, I am the light."

Then you visualize this light surrounding and protecting those you love. With this warm light around and within you sleep peacefully with pleasant dreams.

Chapter 13 – Venusian Ceremonies and Rituals

The following ceremonies and rituals are all done mentally on the astral as we have no need for physical language. I have transformed them to a physical language suited to your understanding and concepts.

The ceremonies are used to symbolize and share feelings within different relationships. They are meant to honor the feeling of special experiences that one wishes to share with one or more. They represent our understanding of relationships and different experiences that a soul encounters – such as love, commitment, honor and even translating or death as you know or understand it.

On Venus I was still too young for those rituals. I have later learned them from Uncle Odin and have now received the permission to make them public.

Venusian Ceremonial Blessing

If you gather with other people for a spiritual event – a workshop, a group meditation, a dinner etc. you may speak the following blessing:

"Our Supreme Creator, we thank you for the energy that flows through us and supports us."

(If also food and drinks are dished than add here the following sentences: "Bless the souls that have served their purpose to serve as nourishment four our physical vehicles to supply us with the energy we need to best represent you. Thank you for the host that prepared this food with love and shares it with us.")

"May we all be grateful to serve as a representative for you and continue to give love as you love us freely. May we all accept the different ways we choose to serve in our chosen ways.

Blessings to all, thanks to all, Omnec (*your* name said here)."

Venusian Love Ritual

Preparation and things needed for love ritual:

▶   A room only to be used for no other reason at this time. The energy must be kept.

▶   One bottle of special wine selected together.

▶   Two wine glasses

▶   Scented body oil selected together.

▶   Each must choose one special flower with fragrance.

▶   Each must choose a special candle – shape and color individual choice.

▶   Each must choose incense with special scent.

The flowers are kept in one vase in the room prepared for the ritual, also the wine, music and two pillows on which to sit.

Bath before entering the room. Use perfume or cologne.

Except the couple that wants to do the love ritual no one else is to enter the room.

The Ritual

First it is important that the two partners have a deep understanding on all levels, knowing that they are souls that have had experiences together before, understanding the quality of unconditioned love, non-personal love that the Creator has given to all living things, the love that supports all that is.

Love is unlimited and exists beyond the limits of each specific existence. Just as love has no boundaries we must extend our energy beyond this temporary physical existence. This ritual is a way to experience this energy and share it with someone special. It must be taken as a serious and very deep love exchange.

It is much easier on the astral where one does not have the limits of a physical body. However, it can be experienced also here in the physical. So I have transferred the information and set down steps to help you to sensitize your physical self as it is a very subtle but deep experience.

First of course there has to be an agreement between the two partners and a commitment to follow the steps together. The ritual takes a total of three days preparation. You must read the passage together so that there is a level of understanding reached. After reading it the first evening you must do a meditation together for thirty minutes:

Visualize all the qualities of each other, seeing the person, loving it, absorbing it into yourself.

After the meditation you look deeply into each other's eyes facing one another, holding hands, feeling the energy and love for one another. Sometimes even pastlife experiences may emerge, whatever emotions are felt must be shared.

Then you both kneel, facing one another, holding hands. You say – the woman first, then the man:

"By Om-Notia-Zedia, I (your name) enter willingly and lovingly into this preparation to share my love energy with you."

Afterwards you embrace holding one another and whisper to each other:

"Amual-San-Tumal" – which means: "I share my essence of love energy with you so we may truly feel and absorb each other's existence."

This is the first step for preparation.

On the second day a fast is necessary – only fruit, juice, herb teas. Each of you has to select a special flower for the other, special incense and a candle. You may purchase these items together or separately. Choose everything carefully and with meaning – even the color of the candles and flowers must have a purpose and meaning. Then buy together a bottle of wine. You must be able to share your meals of fruit together as well. This keeps a necessary bond between you.

Also there is to be no sexual contact for the three days to yourselves or with others. You are in a process of conditioning the senses.

The second evening in privacy and uninterrupted seclusion you select special music to play softly. After bathing and wearing only robes you once again close your eyes and listen to music – concentrating on one another, feeling the love and desire to share your energy with each other.

Then the male lights his chosen candle and says:

"This light represents the fire of love and light that is me. I share it with you."

Then he explains why he chose this candle – the color and what it represents to him. Also he lights his incense, saying:

"This represents my essence that you may breath it consuming and experiencing myself as part of you." – Explain why you chose this particular scent.

The female then lights her candle and says:

"This is my flame of desire and the light that I am, I share it with you." – Explain the choice of color and what it represents.

Then lighting her incense, she says:

"This represents my essence that you may also breath of it consuming and experiencing myself as a part of you." – Explain the scent and why you chose it.

Now you say togehter:

"Our love burns like an eternal light forever. I am filled with it and with your essence."

Now take your flowers and place them between you as you face one another. The female picks up her flower and says:

"This flower represents the delicate and temporary existence of what I now am. Accept it as a token of myself – that even though it be temporary may it exist forever in your memory, its beauty lasting there as a reminder of me."

She gives it to him, explaining why she chose this flower as a representation of herself. He accepts her token.

Then the male gives her his flower, repeating what she has said and explaining why he chose this particular flower as a representation of himself. She accepts his token.

Now you both close your eyes and breath the incense, remembering that it is now the blended essence of both. Then open your eyes and examine the fine quality of your flower, noting every detail and inhale its fragrance. Appreciate its beauty and what it represents. Then look at one another the same way with the same feeling.

Embrace and tell each other how much you appreciate these gifts and one another. Now you may retire.

The third day you consume only fruit, juice and herb tea together for your chosen times for meals. Also meditate together at chosen times if you do more than one meditation a day usually.

Sometime on this day you should enjoy a nature walk together, recognizing that just as all things you see together are God's creation so are you both. Appreciate the wonders of you as unique and beautiful creations. Notice and tell each other what you love about each other. It could be the way you smile, the color of your eyes or hair in the natural light. Hold hands as you walk or walk with arms about each other. Take time to embrace and really kiss deeply. Remember the flower that represents the other. See it in your mind, compare its quality to the quality of the other. Keep this feeling of love and feel the energy of one another. Sit somewhere and each of you with feet touching or crossed. Press your hands together until you feel the heat between your hands. Then turn to your partner and keeping the hands about three inches apart, fingers bent slightly, feel the energy flow between your hands for several moments.

Return home. Share tea or juice. Continue your day. In the evening bath and wear a robe joining one another at the appointed time in the prepared room. Play soft esoteric music. Once again light candles. The female first lights her candle and says:

"This is my flame of desire for you. I have chosen this candle to represent the light that I am." – Then once again explain what the color represents. Then she lights her incense saying:

"This represents my essence that you may inhale it as a part of yourself, that we may become one." – She then seats herself.

The male then lights his candle repeating what the female has said and also his incense, explaining that she may experience his essence as well.

The couple is seated on the floor, facing one another. The female's candle and incense should be on the female's left and the male's one should be on his right. The male should take the flower that the female gave him and express his joy in receiving it and tell her the qualities of her he sees in it, the way its petals feel, the shape, smell and color compared to her when he has finished.

The female also takes the flower the male has given her, expresses the joy and appreciation upon receiving it from him and also appreciates the feel of its petals, the shape, color and smell. Tell why it reminds you of him.

Sit quietly for about five minutes, listen to the music and look at each other, feeling all the love and appreciation for each other. Notice the eyes, breath deeply of the incense, try to distinguish the smell of your partner's incense. Look at the candles, imagine the warmth of each other, see the flame as desire, feel this desire. Can you feel the energy of each other?

The female whispers the male's name and says quietly:

"Amual-San-Tumal. I wish to share my love energy with you, so that we may truly feel and absorb each other's existence."

The male whispers the female's name and repeats what she has said.

Then the male stands up and removes his robe. Then he sits again. The female stands up and removes her robe, then seats herself. Now look at each other, notice each inch of the other's body, remembering love you have shared and how wonderful it was to make love to each other.

Now the woman tells him of one time that she remembers as being wonderful, the stimulating experience first, a time with him somewhere special and why it was special, what he did, how he did it and where it was and why you remember this time.

Then the male also shares a special time of making love with her, where it was, what she did and how she did it and why you remember this time, what made it special.

Now take a few minutes, close your eyes, recall this time and the way you felt. See it with your imagination.

Now the male lies down first on his stomach relaxed. The female kneels on his left side and after rubbing her hands together till they are warm, she acts as if she were sensuously touching his head, arms, back, buttocks, legs, feet – only keeping her hands inches away so only the energy can be felt. Take about six to ten minutes, do it very slowly. Listen to the breathing of each other.

When she has finished she whispers "turn over" – you must not touch each other. She then touches his face, his lips, eyes, every part of the body as if caressing, only with the hands inches away! Do it slowly. When finished she whispers his name and says:

"Now I have shared my love energy with you and I desire the same."

The female then lies on her stomach and the male repeats the same energy treatment with the female repeating what she has said. You must take time and feel the caresses.

Now you both return to your seated position. The male opens the wine, the female holds the glasses. As the male pours he says:

"Take this wine as a representation of my essence and energy that you be fulfilled."

The female says:

"I accept your offering, and these glasses represent my vessel that I may feel your essence."

You toast and drink appreciating the warm feeling and taste, also enjoying the grace and beauty of the bodies God gave you that you may share this feeling.

Tell each other how you would like to touch one another. When you finish the wine you embrace and kiss deeply feeling the flesh of the other as your bodies touch.

Then the male massages scented body oil on the female – front and back, rob and caress. Then the female does the same to the male.

Now have another wine, feel the desire for each other. Now face each other, clasp hands while kneeling. Say: "Amual-San-Tumal." Then say to one another in a whisper:

"I wish to physically make love that I may be fulfilled with your love energy and never forget its existence."

Than you may physically make love, fulfilling the ritual. Enjoy one another completely!

Venusian Commitment Vow

First you and your partner choose the place and time. It is usually done alone. You may also invite others if you choose. It is very personal, not legally binding, only valid for the duration you choose and it can be done more than once throughout your chosen time period together. In other words, it can be renewed as you desire.

Most couples choose a specific selection of music to be played in the background. You can be dressed or undressed. It can be done in a temple, on the beach, in natural surrounding or in the privacy of a home.

The most important factor is that you both choose to make a partnership and share commitment together. Therefore, it can be as individual as you like and for as long as you choose.

There is an exchange of vows and an exchange of tokens representing your love for each other. You choose the objects you exchange. It can be jewelry, crystals, simple stones from a special place you where together. A popular token is a plant. You exchange the tokens and they become symbols of your love and commitment. If you exchange living plants you must give attention that the plant remains healthy and grows as does the relationship, just as your relationship needs nurturing and attention so does the symbol.

If done in natural surroundings any time of day or night is right. Sunset and sunrises are popular as is moonlight. If done indoors a fire place or candles are used, as light or fire is a symbol of purification and spirituality. The moon or sun also serve the purpose and of course you may even have candles outdoors.

After you have chosen a specific place and the tokens of exchange you set the atmosphere – music playing softly, live or recorded. If indoors place three candles in a triangle somewhere in the room. If outdoors in sunlight or moonlight candles are not necessary. If at sunrise or sunset it should be to the left of both partners. If outdoors and you desire candles you should be in the center of the pyramid of candles. If indoors with a fire place the fire should also be to the left of the partners who will be facing one another. If using candles placed in the room the one lone candle should be to the left (see diagram).

candle

couple

candle   candle

First you walk slowly toward one another in the prepared place, carrying your token or symbol in the left hand.

When you are about one foot apart stop, facing one another. You look deeply into one another's eyes, hands in front, left hand with token palm up, right hand palm up supporting the left hand.

As you look in one another's eyes the female first speaks as she symbolizes the emotional or feeling one. She says:

"I (your name) am here to offer you (his name; first name only) this symbol of my love, devotion and desire to share my energy with you." Hold toward him the token. Then he reaches with his right hand and takes your offering, placing gift and his right hand next to his heart. He says:

"I accept this symbol and all it means, I take it into my heart and shall so honor and care for it and all it stands for." – (She stands with both hand's palms up.) He then says:

"I (his name) offer you (her name) this symbol of my love, devotion and desire to share my energy with you." – He holds out his left hand with token toward her. She with her right hand takes the token to her heart. She replies:

"I accept this symbol and all it means, I take it into my heart and shall so honor and care for it and all it stands for."

Both kneel, still facing one another, still looking into the other's eyes and place the tokens on the ground of the floor between them. They clasp one another's hands. Then they both say slowly together:

"I shall love you unconditionally as the Creator intended it. I shall share my life and all it creates with you. I will accept you as you are and grow with you. We shall be as one even separated. Our love is there. It is."

Then they stand still clasping hands. She places his left hand on her heart. He does the same. Both together say:

"We vow devotion, love and commitment to share love and honor one another. We will inspire each other and support that which we choose, until the time comes that our souls go their way. Without regret we shall still remember all that we have shared. We will still love and honor all that we are. It is."

Then facing the candle or the fire or the sunset etc. to the left you hold each other's right hand. You look at the symbol of light and say:

"May we walk together now and forever as friends. Let the light surround and protect us and all that we love, bonding us that we may be as one. May we live according to the Om Notia Vidya (Laws of the Supreme Deity). The symbols we exchanged shall be a reminder of what we are and mean to one another. It is and we are. Amual abactu baraka bashad (universal love and blessing)."

The couple faces one another, embracing and exchanging energy. Of course they may kiss. Then sit on the floor, drink wine and admire each other's tokens.

Friends may be invited afterwards or the next day for celebration. The couple must take care of their tokens for they are a symbol of your vows.

Concepts of Relationships (with Commitments)

There are different types of relationship. One type is where you do not communicate or share and build walls around yourselves and stay together for appearances and only live in the same house each negating the other's feelings. (You tolerate each other but grow apart.)

Another type of commitment is where you cannot accept the other's desires or forgive them for misunderstandings or mistakes. This one needs flare ups and violent outbursts to bring you together in apologizes and guilt over things done and said. (You are on a happy and angry rollercoaster, bound to separate.)

The last type is the best one. It is one where you share everything and accept the differences between you and care about the desires. It takes trust, honesty and sharing – being able to understand the mistakes and forgive. Communication is important. (You accept each other and the relationship is strong.)

Venusian Healing and Cleaning of negative Energy for Environment

Sometimes even on other dimensions you encounter unwanted negative energy or entities. Sometimes they are left over from previous situations by former souls or there are the lower astral entities that will use the less aware being as a means of controlling and manipulation.

Unfortunately, many such entities wait for opportunities to utilize unaware beings who open themselves up for channeling. Also the desire for psychic experiences may provide a means of entry into your own existence. Sometimes it is only accumulated energy or a left over wandering soul, confused by his or her last moments in the physical, especially if it was traumatic or so sudden that their minds did not have time to register what happened in many sudden or violent situations. Also you will encounter many souls who are so attached to their former situation that they have trouble realizing or accepting the transition necessary for their own progress and will hang around and try to communicate with whom ever enters their former domain.

You can also encounter evil forces drawn by unaware persons dabbling in black magic or physical phenomena or entities. The souls are trapped because they are unaware of their own fate! However, all souls or entities should be free to take the place where they should be placed.

These wandering souls are former residents of a special place and may have experienced a traumatic or sudden death therefore making it hard for them to be aware that they should depart.

Entities on the other hand are an accumulation of negative energy enforced by the own energy field of living beings. For instance if one is interested in manipulation or is controlling others by the use of their energy they draw energy from the negative forces that are built and accumulated out of murder, hate, resentment and vengeance.

These are very powerful forms of energy representing the negative existence of our emotions. These are created by any human being who generates this energy out of personal frustration and anger. It accumulates in the lower astral and can be drawn upon by anyone who is destructive. Sometimes this energy is so strong it can appear as a demon or destructive energy. It is very powerful, usually because the soul that generates it is very new and unaware of the power of our thoughts and the energy that one soul can generate. Once this energy is emitted and drawn directly by another negativity generating energy it accumulates and then is re-utilized by the souls with the strongest desire and force or will.

Sometimes young people on earth who are very emotional and have not yet reached the sexual age for releasing of emotional energy are apt to draw upon this energy in their frustration at being in between innocence and promiscuity. These occurrences are related to as poltergeists. It is an unconscious act on behalf of the young person but because they have no real outlet for emotions and have built up energy due to lack of understanding of meditation or protection they are apt to draw this energy from other dimensions in situations that create confusion or anger and resentment. Therefore, they can create havoc in their own homes or environment without knowing that they himself are the cause.

Souls that are trapped in any dimension or in the physical plane are only confused former residents that either do not know that their physical bodies are now no longer inhabitable because their deaths were so sudden, such as accident or war victims. Also it could be that their deaths were so painful – either emotionally or physically such as suicide, murder, or that they had some unfulfilled desire or attachment here that they really cannot leave or accept their own departure. Sometimes in the case of torture or murder they may continually reenact their last hour or moments. However, they are caught in a trap of their own emotions – whether it be attachment, fear or rage. They all need to be made aware and freed.

If you feel that you have such entities or souls in your living space, there are steps you can take. However, do not become paranoid and feel that every place you are is full of such energy. This is an obsession and being fanatical or focusing on such energy at all times is completely uncalled for. You do not have to search for trouble. Only be aware if you are uncomfortable or sleepless or have reoccurring unaccounted for occurrences that keep happening. However, it is not necessary to cleanse every room you enter or search for such happenings. Then you begin to look like a fanatic (which you are) and people will avoid you. Also you may draw these negative energies unto yourself because you are putting so much attention on them! Remember where your attention goes your energy flows! So to constantly be on the look out for trouble you can actually create it.

Now what can we do in these special rare cases? Well, if you are of a specific religion you can approach your pastor, priest or clergyman to see if help is available from there. If you get turned down then you may work on your own.

You need to open all windows in your apartment, home or whatever building the disturbances are occurring. Then get incense of sandalwood, incense and myrrh. Bring some in every room. In the main doorway into the place make a pyramid by placing white, pink, green candles in a triangle in front of the door. You should have three people altogether including yourself as helpers. You need the three candles mentioned above placed at all entrances or exits of the home – not windows.

Make sure each room has wood, metal, water, earth and fire. Check each room. Toilet is water, flowers and plants are earth, faucets are considered as water, metal or mineral. (What stands for wood?) Also colors representing each will work – silver for metal, or rust, yellow or red for fire, brown or black for earth, and green, white, blue or purple for water. (What stands for wood?)

Now unplug all electrical appliances. Then you and two friends or more but at least three must sit in the central location in a triangle in the center of the room. Join hands and chant HU for at least twelve times. Sit quietly for ten minutes and see the environment filled with blue-white purifying light. Then hands joined stand up and say:

"You unwanted and misplaced force, be gone, this is now... place (Say the name of whom ever is to reside or work there). You must be informed that you no longer should be here and must go to where you were meant to go or return to the energy that created you. In the name of the greatest force of all, the One Divine Creator – I (or other name) now reside here and shall not welcome you in this present form. Be gone, be what you were intended and be free of what has drawn you. You are not part of this place anymore. Bless you and may you find the way that was meant for you."

Then each present takes a room. Stand in the center of the room. Take three deep breaths, imagine as you breath in you are filling yourself with pure blue-white energy and as you exhale it destroys all negative forces and clears the room. Chant three times "A-Lah-ya". Then holding your arms over your head you turn in small circles counterclock-wise around the whole circumference of the room. When you return to your original spot turn clockwise in the other direction. See that as you spin you gather all the negative energy around you. Now walk to the center of the room. Close your eyes, hold your hands up and see it in your mind swirling away into infinity like a tornado and being absorbed into the ocean of love and mercy and dissipating and returning as pure energy, free of the burdens of hate, fear, resentment, frustration and destruction. See how it is being pulled off you like a soiled garment and swirling away to become clean and pure.

After you visualize this and it is repeated in every room by one of you you sit once again in the main room, hold hands and say:

"Now it is a free place, clean of all old energy. Thank you, Supreme One. All is done."

Preparation for Cleaning of Environment

1. Select all tools needed for preparation.
2. Prepare each room.
3. Choose all to participate – three or more persons, not more than seven.
4. Open all windows to allow energy to enter and leave.
5. Do meditation in the entrance of the main room of environment.
6. Perform the ceremony in each room.
7. Rejoin in the same room as beginning to give thanks to the Supreme Being.

There are always seven steps as it is a spiritual number on Venus.

Tools needed: Participants, Incense, Three candles – white for spirituality, pink for love and green for healing, representatives for water, earth, fire and minerals or corresponding colors: blue, red, orange, brown, black, yellow or green.

Venusian Ceremony for the Transition of Dimension

Venusian Understanding of death

Before I will start to describe the Venusian Ceremony for the transition of dimension or death, as you call it, let me explain to you our understanding of death.

Unlike you of Earth we of Venus look at what you call death as a transition from one existence to another or the ascension to a higher existence. So death is for us more a joyful event, a kind of graduation from the limited to a less limited kind of existence. Also unlike those of Earth all Venusians know their destiny of existence and are prepared when the time comes to leave the place where they formerly existed. Sometimes mates are born around the same time and likewise all transcend together!

Venusians also do not have the aging process that the physical beings encounter. In the physical after we manifest a body we can live 500 of your years and on Venus several thousand years. It is not as long as you think if you allow yourself to overcome the limited concept of earth time. As the soul is immortal we really live eternity, so what is a few thousand years!

So as you can see our concept of time is different as is our concept of death. The only thing that changes is the location of your next existence and that is based on what you have learned in a particular life existence. Then your soul manifests wherever it should be according to what is yet to be learned and what has been learned or fulfilled. And as we are all truly individual this place can be very different from soul to soul and be located within one of the many universes, planets and dimensions that one can exist on!

We do not see our passing as something sad or feel loss because we know as soul they still exist and our relation to them changes from life to life. When you understand and know these things it is easier not to form attachments to each other or to animals and things. We know that we own nothing, we only use what we need, but all belongs to the Supreme One. All that is, is soul – that is all that that we can control.

When you are controlled by others or by circumstances it is usually due to the influence of a particular lifetime and accepting the circumstances, concepts and beliefs of the world in which one is placed. This happens because if you are physical you have a physical body and a new brain and in learning to adopt you loose the memories of what or where you were before. It does not help if the people who are your peers are not spiritually aware and are also caught up in their existence and have also forgotten. Books like these and others that intend to reinform people about their universal origin are a way to break the cycle and prepare people to understand themselves as soul.

Now the people on Venus or any other of the places existing in the dimensions above the physical have a big advantage. Because we do not have to deal with a new body and brain out of physical material or deal with the shock of being physically born, our memories of previous lives and experiences are not deeply affected nor are our memories buried in the subconscious as it is with a soul that incarnates through a physical birth. Therefore, we are able to adjust to our new environment with less struggle than those in the physical.

However, you do not only have to adjust to a physical body but have to learn a language and are exposed to many emotional conflicts. That is why the physical existences are so valuable – and there are many thousands of lives you as soul spend there. It is a necessary preparation. When one learns to overcome all the conditioning and is able to see beyond it and develop a soul understanding then you are at the end of your physical incarnations and are well prepared to learn at the higher levels. Therefore, we must make an effort to learn all we can, knowing that we never know all!

Knowing the Life Plan

We all choose our life cycle before entering, knowing the timespan we shall exist, knowing our purpose and karmic involvement with other souls. This is true for all souls – even the ones born into the physical. However, with the struggle here in the physical, with encounters with strong emotions and with the complexity of the physical learning process, much of the memory of the previous existence and of the choice we made, the details and length of life and the way it shall end are almost forgotten.

If our parents or guardians here were to remind us that we were souls, that we came here out of choice for whatever reason, it would be easier to remember and overview what lies ahead.

Last year I learned of a very rare case where a young girl remembered her life plan. In a TV documentary there was a story of a family in California – a mother, father and their two daughters. The oldest daughter became fascinated with angels around age 13. She also began to tell her family that she did not have long to be with them here on earth! They did not want to believe this of course. However, the girl continued and insisted that they be prepared.

The parents were not too concerned as she was not depressed or occupied with any suicidal tendencies. However, she began to study esoteric books and to collect stories, books and calendars about angels, as well all sorts of angel pictures and models. She even baked special cookies at Christmas – angel cookies. As well she had taken on an angelic appearance and grew concerned with helping others who were depressed or unhappy. She accomplished all she set out to do. She graduated with honors, sang in the school- and church choir. When anyone asked her about her intentions for college or a carrier she would say: 'I will then not be here anymore.' 'How can you say this?' they would ask. 'Because I know that I only chose to be here for a short time', was her answer.

When she was 18 her prom came – a dance celebration for highschool graduates, the first formal occasion for young people, one, every girl looks forward to, as you get to dress like a princess going to a ball. She had her prom and a handsome excort and was happy! Then, in the automobile drive home there was an accident: Out of six people in the car she was the only one killed.

101

Her family was sad. While going through her belongings in her room they found a letter, dated the day before her death:

Dear Mom, Dad and family:

Do not cry over me. I am fine for my time here is done and I shall have to leave. I will always be near in spirit and we will all reunite when your time on earth is finished as well. I had a wonderful life – friends, a beautiful home and a loving family. For this I am thankful. We each choose our family and time. Love knows no boundaries or limits. It can always be felt and experienced. Take care of my angel collection!

Love you

Angela

The family cried and hugged each other and upon returning downstairs found a fresh baked angel cookie on a plate in the kitchen – still warm! They knew it was from her a sign that she was ever near. In her honor they opened a store that sells everything to do with angels.

However, stories like this doe not often occur. More often any memory or the ability to remember or even communicate with unmaterial friends is discouraged and often dismissed as a child's fantasy. As the soul, now as a child, is expected to respect its parents and elders, it begins to doubt or become inhibited to discuss or share these experiences – because of lack of understanding by most people here or a fear of being ridiculed and feeling separated and not accepted. So these memories become dull or buried in the subconscious.

There is so much wisdom and knowledge that every soul has, that it is wonderful to be able to reawaken these memories. That is what I and others like myself are here for – to change the consciousness and perception and allow more truth and the past existence to be experienced by each soul, so that they may accept their universal existence! So I hope that in the future we have more aware parents who accept their children as souls in their care, and help them to retain this experience and knowledge while they are living with them! This will be the beginning of the New Age of the earth.

On Venus and as I said on any dimension above the physical these memories of the soul are always recognized and nourished by those around it as it enters its life cycle there. Because you are incarnating on a higher, more aware level without divisions and without the many diverse consciousnesses that you have in a multicultural planet such as earth or planets like earth in other universes. Remember, there has to be in each solar system or universe one physical planet that is divided and full of confused and misinformed beings. This is necessary, because as we are struggling through a maze we are able to complete and overcome our experiences there. So eventually the soul can say – yes, I have been there, yes, I have done that! Then it begins to see without the divisions and learns to live without judgement and overcomes the confusion, fear and anger, and learns to accept and love life and all it has to offer – not fearing death – but seeing it as a chance to overcome limitations and to graduate to a higher place of learning.

Because we lack aggression, fear and much suffering on Venus as we have all graduated we step above these experiences. We do not encounter accidental or traumatic death situations. Of course we love and care and form families and communities and share an emotional attachment to others. We also have learned that every separation in every life cycle – be it physical or otherwise – is only temporarily for we are immortal and never cease to be.

So we joyfully help the soul on its journey as they progress, knowing we shall miss them as we have shared our lives with them, but keeping their memory alive within our soul, looking forward to reuniting with them elsewhere as I have experienced this here on earth. The meeting of old soul friends, residing in new bodies and new situations – how joyfully it is to have them sometimes recognize me! Then I know that indeed I am not a stranger here on earth, only an old friend, sharing and encountering and reuniting with all my old soul buddies! Then when our life here is done we can rejoice and be happy to have finished some very difficult lessons and have shared much joy and beauty – knowing that this is not life's end, only the beginning of a new existence!

Example: My Venusian mother Shawik knew that upon my birth she would complete her particular life existence on Teutonia and finish her relation to myself and her family there. My father Deashar had difficulty with this but knew it was to be accepted. He also knew hat he would continue his work and would not have the time to contribute the care I needed. All this was known at the beginnings of that life cycle before their souls entered this existence.

My parents had a long life before my birth. I was too young to participate in my mother's transition ceremony. But all was known and chosen by each soul before it came to be.

Usual there is always an underlying touch of sadness at parting, but his is natural as we become attached to others. It is a lesson to learn to overcome, to find joy in the benefits, to share in the advancement of those we love and not make it difficult for the passing soul to leave because of our own selfish desire to keep them with us.

As I have said no matter what dimension on which the soul exists there are still lessons to learn and difficulties to overcome. Even if a place is considered in comparison to physical standards to heaven like or fairy tale in appearance there are always different types of difficulties to overcome!

The Ceremony

There is a special temple on Venus for the ceremony. It looks like gleaming crystal. It has three steps leading into it. The three steps stand for the three states of man's consciousness. The first and lowest step stands for the causal nature of man, the second step is the mental process and the third step is for the spiritual development sometimes known as the trial.

Then there are three arched doorways – the center one for the person who is to make the transition, the left one for all the Venusians who wish to participate in the ceremony, the right one for the spiritual teachers and higher masters.

First as you enter, the radiance of light is very bright. It takes a moment for the eyes to adjust. Then in the center is a raised square platform with seven stairs leading up to it. The seven steps represent the seven divine laws of the Supreme Deity, the laws you must live in order to be advanced enough to participate in the ceremony.

There is a large circle surrounding the platform about 50 feet in circumference. It is made of pure red gleaming crystal and there are bands of gold encircling that with a band about two feet of pure white crystal in between the two gold bands which are about one foot each. This circle is surrounded by three rows of benches, each row containing four seats. You can see also on the outer edge just beyond the last gold band all the zodiac symbols, some familiar to earth and some more ancient.

Above the platform in the domed ceiling is a circle of large round different colored crystal lights, each one representing the zodiac symbols of Venus. Venus has 13, Earth twelve. Each planet has its own number of symbols. Unlike Earth our symbols do not represent animals but the energy that controls and supports our planet.

The platform is gold and so are the seven steps. As the Venusians enter there is complete silence. All sit in deep meditation focusing their energy on the one to ascend the platform. Then you can hear a faint singsong music and feel the energy intensify. You notice all the thirteen circular crystal lights beginning to glow and shine on top the cubic like platform. You also see beams of light from each Venusian sitting around the circle. They are generating the energy with their concentration to enable the gateway to appear for the transition.

As the pleasant sound grows stronger along with the beams of multicolored lights on top of the cube you see a flame of many colors appear on top of the platform. As it grows to about ten feet in height you then see the one who is to transcend. Slowly and with much grace and dignity he or she approaches the stairs and walks into the flame.

Slowly the flame and pulsating lights along with the sound dies down. Silently the Venusians walk out of the temple with a contended look of joy and inspiration on their faces. The ceremony is completed. This is repeated for each individual who is to transcend from the astral Venus.

Chapter 14 – Test and Initiation for potential Star Seed People

𝕸 any souls have been incarnating on Earth for the past 100 years or so for specific purposes. These are elder souls. Many have been residing on other planets and systems to be prepared to help with the New Age on earth. We call them star seeds or star children. Many of you reading this are such souls. Many have no idea why there are attracted to stories about UFOs or beings from other planets because it contradicts what they have learned or believe to exist. However, they continue to search for answers. I have prepared a questionnaire to help you decide if you are a star seed or star child.

But this is not a test to assume that one individual is greater than another, for this would inflate egos or create a feeling of superiority which I discourage.

It is a test to help each individual understand their own particular sensitivities or attraction to certain objects that one on the journey from creation to this moment has carried via soul from past experiences in incarnations throughout this vast universe and others. For indeed most of us are star seeds having existed thousands of life cycles elsewhere. It is only to make you aware of the universal connection we all have and to open your conscious mind to the unlimited possibilities that you as soul have experienced and to give you the ability to find the way that your destiny has prepared for you.

It is important to become participants, not observers. This you test yourself and seek answers to guide you and reconnect perhaps lost feelings and memories. For there are few souls here that are here for the first time, and you who are aware enough to be interested in a book like this or any material to raise the consciousness and increase the knowledge and truth of the existence of one's divine self outside this single life existence, are not here for the first time and indeed are not new souls. You are the ones preparing the way for old souls to take their proper place in guiding the younger souls and making sure that this knowledge shall be available for them and that this earth shall still exist for their much needed experiences!

We are all star seeds – and citizens of more than one universe and part of a never ceasing powerful essence. The only difference between you and younger souls is that you know from where you came and where you are heading – and not still seeking. We all are creators of our own existence.

Now, the pattern profile of star people contains the following elements. Check those to which you relate:

1. Unusual blood type   yes O no O

2. Lower body temperature   yes O no O

3. Low blood pressure   yes O no O

4. Extra or transitional vertebrae   yes O no O

5. Check areas in which you are hypersensitive:

   pain .... yes O   no O

   light .... yes O   no O

   touch .... yes O   no O

   smell .... yes O   no O

   hearing....................... yes O   no O

   taste .... yes O   no O

   emotion .... yes O   no O

6. Do you require

   much sleep.................... yes O   no O

   or little sleep? .... yes O   no O

7. Were you   yes O   no O

   a favorite child?................ yes O   no O

   an unliked child? .... yes O   no O

8. Did you suffer from chronic sinusitis? yes O   no O

9. Do you suffer from

   swollen and painful joints? .... yes O   no O

   headaches brought on by humidity? yes O   no O

a severe pain in the back of your neck? yes O no O

10. Did you feel your father and mother were not your true
    parents?   yes O no O

    Have you often felt that your true ancestors came
    from another world? .... yes O no O

    Have you often yearned for a place you consider to
    be your true home? .... yes O no O

11. Do you experience a feeling of great urgency in which
    you feel you only have a short time to complete import-
    ant though often not clearly realized goals?

    .... yes O no O

12. Did you have unseen friends as a child? yes O no O

13. Do you often hear whines, a click, or buzzing sounds
    preceding or during psychic event?   yes O no O

14. Check which applies to you:

    I do my best physical labor in the day and my best
    mental labor at night............. yes O no O

    I do my best physical labor at night and my best
    mental labor in the day........... yes O no O

15. Did it seem as though you had unusual natural abilities
    for any of the following:

    art .... yes O no O

music .... yes O no O

mathematics .... yes O no O

healing .... yes O no O

acting .... yes O no O

inventions.................... yes O no O

16. Have you ever been told you have unusual or compelling
    eyes?   yes O no O

17. Check those items to which you seem to have a more
    than normal attraction:

willow trees .... yes O no O

humming birds .... yes O no O

eagles .... yes O no O

rocks.......................... yes O no O

stars .... yes O no O

lilacs .... yes O no O

natural crystals .... yes O no O

mushrooms .... yes O no O

darkness....................... yes O no O

electrical storms .... yes O no O

nature . . . . yes O no O

the name Leah or Lia (Leeah) . . . . . . yes O no O

18. Do you feel any sort of attachment to the planet Venus?   yes O no O

19. Is it true or not that you seem to become "empath" taking on the problems, feelings, pains of those around you?   yes O no O

20. Do you often see a bright light even when your eyes are closed?   yes O no O

21. Have you received the message from your guidance "Now is the time"?   yes O no O

22. Are you attracted to the constellation

Sirus . . . . yes O no O

Drago . . . . yes O no O

others (please indicate which). . . . .

. . . .

23. Do you believe in reincarnation?   yes O no O

If you feel that you remember one or more past lives, indicate in which countries they were and in which time period they transpired: . . . .

. . . .

. . . .

If you have a pet indicate the type and its breed: . . . .

. . . .

24.   State your favorite preference of

music . . . . yes ○   no ○

books . . . . yes ○   no ○

movies . . . . yes ○   no ○

television viewing . . . . yes ○   no ○

and what makes you laugh the most: . . . .

. . . .

. . . .

25.   State your attitude toward death:

. . . .

. . . .

. . . .

26.   Have you ever taken hallucinogenic or psychotropic
drugs?   yes ○   no ○

27.   State in brief the event that occurred to you around
the age of five. Tell who or what you saw. Share your
message if any was given:

. . . .

. . . .

. . . .

28. State in brief the event that occurred to you at around age eleven that altered your life style or attitudes:

. . . .

. . . .

. . . .

29. If you have maintained contact with any entity or entities, how is contact made?

. . . .

. . . .

. . . .

30. What do your entities look like?

. . . .

. . . .

. . . .

31. What type of messages do you receive?

. . . .

. . . .

. . . .

32. When do you feel the following events will take place:

Pole shift . . . .

global famine ....

War III ....

Armageddon ....

world wide UFO contacts ....

New Age ....

the first earth changes ....

If you mentally answered the questions or if you took the trouble to write down answers on a separate sheet – you might be interested in noting that if you felt that all the questions related directly to you that you are indeed a star seed or star child. If only half the questions related to you then you are a star helper. If only a third, then you are obviously fascinated by our work and desire to change the consciousness and help expand knowledge.

Star seeds are most sensitive to light, touch and emotion. Equally divided is the need for much or little sleep. Only some of the star seeds feel that they were favorite children, most of them feel that their father or mother are not their true parents. Many are troubled by chronic sinusitis. Some suffer from swollen and painful joints and/or must endure pain in the back of the neck, and many are affected by higher humidity. Almost all of them insist that they have yearned for a place they consider their true home. Many experience a feeling of great urgency and envision themselves as working against some cosmic time table in order to complete important goals. More than three third of them hear whines, buzzing or clicking during psychic events.

The star seeds are overwhelming night people. Most of them indicate they prefer doing their important mental work after sun dawn. Also most feel pronounced abilities – to music, mathematics, healing, acting or to inventions.

Many of them have compelling or unusual eyes and consider themselves as empaths. Your affinity with eagles, crystals, rocks, willow trees, stars, electrical storms are symbolic and represent memories of freedom – flexible relationships and deep understanding of themselves in relation to nature and all things.

The name Leah or Lia surfaces again and again and has meaning to about half of the star seeds. Most of them often see bright lights when their eyes are closed. The greatest response of star seeds is to the constellation of Sirius.

Not all star seeds claim to remember specific past lives but all of them believe in reincarnation. The most past life remembrances are Egypt, then England or revolutionary France or Israel. All star seeds love pets. Classical music is most popular of star seeds. More than half of them prefer metaphysical books and science fiction books as the second choice. Correspondingly they prefer science fiction movies, but some also like comedies. Their sense of humor tends to be satirical in nature. Television choices rate as documentations and talk shows and science fiction movies.

An amazing number of star seeds have resisted the highly popularized hallucinogenic drugs. Most of them have never tried any drugs. Also most star seeds had an activating vision at age five and some have endured a traumatic event at around age eleven. The great majority of them have maintained at least a sporadic contact with a guiding entity and have continued to receive messages and visions at various times in their lives. Not all star seeds feel endowed with the gift of prophecy.

The difference between those who bear the star seed and those who do not is that star people are aware that they are citizens of more than one universe, more than one level of being, more than one dimensional essence.

Initiation: Spiritual Journey

*L*et us cease with a spiritual exercise. It is helpful for awakening your feeling of oneness with your true existence and memories of the greater self.

Prepare for a journey: Lie down in a quiet and darkened room. Meditation music is helpful, also incense.

Close your eyes and picture yourself breathing in pure, cleansing air. Visualize it entering your left nostril, imagine the air filtering through your brain, through all your thoughts, throughout your entire body, picking up any and all darkness and negativity, all body impurities. Visualize that darkness leaving through your right nostril, in through the left cleansing purifying air and out through the right.

Imagine the air that comes out of your right nostril being dark at first, then becoming gradually brighter as it cleanses your entire being, both mentally and physically. With continual slow, rhythmic breathing the air will become gradually clean.

Breathe in clean air and out clean air until a cycle, round and round, in and out is formed. Continue this until approximately ten minutes of breathing has taken place.

Now imagine yourself venturing forth on your spiritual journey, berobed in pure shining, protective white light. Begin walking slowly, purposefully through an enchanted forest.

You are following a golden light, and you are treading a path lined with beautiful trees of all types, sizes and varieties.

See the branches of the trees. They are very low, low enough to reach and to touch. You are able to touch them without straying from the straight path, two feet wide, that leads you through the forest.

Look at the back of the tree, although some of the trees have rough, exterior bark, you are able to see the soft, inner core beneath which gives off a glow where the life force exists.

Continue walking and look to your left. Beside the path sits a small bearcat. It is friendly and playful. Reach down and pet it and watch it respond lovingly.

Walk on following the golden light. Ahead is a beautiful lake, filled with sparkling, clean water, which comes from a mountain stream. The lake nurtures multicolored lively fish, and it enters out into the ocean of life.

As you stand before the pulsating ocean of life reach into your robe, just over the heart, and remove a drinking cup that rests there – your cup.

Hold it heavenwards and physically, mentally shout up the words: "Love! Love! Love!"

As you watch the sky above you, you see a beautiful love vibration gathering from the four corners of the heavens. One bright ray of light comes from the north, another one from the south, another from the east and again one from the west.

They meet, merge and form one almost blinding ray of white light.

This ray is filled with heavenly love from the angelic beings, and is beaming down to you. It is splashing into your cup, filling it as it transforms itself from light to a milky pink nectar.

It flows into your cup until it runs over the brim and anoints you.

Now lower the cup to your lips and drink the nectar. Drink it all. Drink down this delicious heavenly love, which bears an apricot like taste. Feel how it glows and warms every part of your body.

Look at your cup. See how it has changed. Look within it and without. See how is has been transformed from holding this heavenly love. Put your cup back inside your robe and enjoy the warmth in your body.

This is your first step to awareness. Next you feel yourself begin to float. You are rising higher and higher.

As you look up, you see a huge glowing cloud descending to meet you. It is white, tinged with gold. You rise higher. It comes nearer. When you reach it you climb aboard and rise even higher.

You are rising above the Earth. You are rising above the clouds. You are rising higher and higher.

You move beyond the Earth, beyond the stars, beyond this dimension, moving through many levels of various colors to reach the beautiful crystal city in the sky.

Step off the cloud and see before you a crystal river of cleansing, sacred holy water. This holy healing water cleanses within as well as without. It removes all scars, hurts, pains, regrets, burdens, and leaves you clean.

Wash yourself. Dip your whole body into the water. It has a perfect temperature and it only rises as high as your heart.

Watch as troublesome annoying habits, addictions and problems float away. Then clean and pure get out and walk to the opposite shore.

This is the second step.

This is the time to make a decision without regret. If you have a problem you wish to solve, a decision to make, leave it also floating on the water.

As you stand on the opposite shore see these things bobbing on the top of the water. Now you are facing these problems, you are detached, separated from them. You have severed the emotional attachment to you. Face the problems and say this:

"In the name of God, if it is for my good or gain, rise! In the name of God, if it is not, then let it sink from me!"

If the problem rises return to the water, snatch it from the air and clutch it to your bosom. It is for your good and gain.

You may always test the problem again in the same manner to see if you must continue to carry this.

If the problem sinks and is gone let it be. It is not for you as you have made your decision and have completed the test.

You must turn away from the river and climb the grassy hill in front of you.

As you climb toward the top, program yourself positively. Be truly proud of your effort toward self-improvement. Vow to move away from any negative, unwanted habits.

Now at the top of the hill you see a beautiful golden chalice, encrusted with jewels. The huge chalice is filled with a golden substance. It is the distillation of the highest love available – unconditional love. This love will transform you, for it is even above that of heavenly love. It is directly from the source of all that is.

You have been filled with heavenly angelic love, you have cleansed yourself in the crystal river, washing yourself within and without. You have made any necessary decision with divine help. Now drink from the golden chalice of the Creator's love. Drink every drop. Vow to be from this moment on a source of unconditional love yourself.

Whenever you interact with any living thing, picture yourself as being filled with their love and it flowing from you to persons, animals, plants. It flows through the top of your head and fills you continually. It is always replenished.

As you finish drinking from the chalice, set it down and look toward the horizon. See there a beautiful crystal city and in the midst looming up the golden spires of a golden temple. You rush to the temple. You are now prepared to enter its vibration.

See a gigantic door nine feet high, three feet wide. It is open. Enter and discover the three highest vibrations: love, wisdom and knowledge.

Awaiting you are your higher self, your guardian angel, your spiritual guide and master. You will learn your true purpose on Earth. You will remember your mission. If there are past life remembrances in connection to your present you will learn of them here.

All you learn will be for your good and your gain. These will prepare you for your birth in the stars. This is your star birth.

Now return fulfilled and ready.

Image Directory

Publisher's Recommendations

Venus Pearls

From Venus I Came
Omnec Onec

Omnec Onec was born on the astral level of the planet Venus and came to Earth with her own physical body in 1955. She tells about the history, spirituality and culture of the Venusians, who once were a physical society and who have lived on the astral plane for a long time. Omnec tells about her first years of life on the astral Venus, explains why and how she came to Earth and what mission she has to fulfill here. This book is a unique document of its kind about the fabulous world of the astral. Being a sister planet to Earth, Venus has already gone through a similar process of transformation into a higher frequency plane as the Earth and its inhabitants are currently going through.

The history of Venus, delivered through Omnec Onec, along with its spiritual teachings, are a gift of pure love and show how the transformation into an expanded consciousness can be mastered in accordance with the universal laws of the Supreme Deity.

This book is the authorized re-publication of the original version as written by Omnec Onec in the 1960s and first published in the USA in 1991 under the title UFO – From Venus I Came.

New Release 2023, DISCUS Publishing
ISBN: 978-3-910804-09-8

Angels Don't Cry

Omnec Onec

Angels Don't Cry is the stunning sequel to Omnec Onec's autobiography **"From Venus I Came"**. This book is about the earthly life of the Venusian. Difficult family circumstances, constant changes of location and a spiritually unawakened environment presented very challenging conditions for the conscious child from Venus. The telepathic and sometimes physical contact with her friends and relatives from Venus as well as the awareness of her mission gave Omnec the strength to endure this life and to master it in love. Slowly, Omnec's way to the public was paved and the fulfillment of her mission as an Ambassador of Venus took hold with the first publication of her life story by Lt. Col. Ret. Wendelle C. Stevens in 1991.

New Release 2023, DISCUS Publishing
ISBN: 978-3-910804-10-4

Handbook of Venusian Spirituality

Omnec Onec

Essence of Spiritual Teachings

The truth is always simple. Practical and current, Omnec writes about the essence of creation, Soul, and life. This volume contains the essential message of the Venusian and gives practical keys for the expansion of consciousness.

New Release 2023, DISCUS Publishing
ISBN: 978-3-910804-11-1

The Venusian Trilogy
Contents:
"From Venus I Came" – Autobiography Part 1
A classic in spiritual literature: In her autobiography, Omnec Onec portrays her *life on the astral level of Venus* and teaches *timeless wisdom*. She speaks about the adventure of how and why she decided to manifest a physical body, and about her journey to Earth in 1955. This book was first published by the US Col. Wendelle C. Stevens in 1991.

"Angels Don't Cry" – Autobiography Part 2
In the continuation of her autobiography, Omnec tells her experiences on Earth.

"My Message" – Essence of spiritual teachings. Omnec writes about the essence of creation, Soul, and life. This part also contains a chapter about the evolution of Souls on Earth.

Note: This edition contains all of Omnec's three books and was compiled and in some parts revised by her supporter and deceased previous publisher Kouki Wohlwend in 2012.
544 pages with colored pictures
ISBN: 978-3-9523815-2-6

Simply Wisdom and Love – Venusian Spirituality
Omnec Onec and Anja Schäfer
The world as we know it is changing rapidly, the Transformation Process of the Earth is in progress. The current world system, in which a few powerful people control and manipulate others, is coming to an end. The Earth is ascending to a higher frequency. Thanks to courageous messengers such as

Omnec Onec, we are reminded of what we have long forgotten: that our ancestors came from other star systems and galaxies. Our existence is not limited to the physical life we live. We are all Souls and universal beings, created by a loving Creator.

Contents: The Unknown History of our Solar System and the ongoing Transformation of the Earth from Venusian perspective · "The True Story of Christ" · "A Venusian Letter" · Transcripts of Omnec's public appearances with Q&A · Project Omnec's Oasis – a Place to live in Harmony with the Universe

Loving, wise, inspiring. This book is a light focus for the expansion of consciousness and gives a deep insight into the teachings of the Venusians.

DISCUS Publishing, 2016
ISBN: 978-3-9817441-0-1

Venus and I
Anja Schäfer
My Journey of Coming to Remembrance of my Soul Mission
— 25 years with Omnec Onec —
A Story about Initiations, the Transformation of the Earth, and Love

"This book describes the author's spiritual awakening process. Her refreshing and witty way of writing made me feel like I was along on her journey."
Axel

Contents: *Contents:* Venus Ambassadors, Omnec Onec, Dr. Raymond Keller "Cosmic Ray", Phaistos Disc, Atlantis, Cyclic Time – Linear Time, Venus-Germany-Connection, Transformation and Future of the Earth, Ascension, Awakening, Artificial Timeline (2D) and Natural Timeline (5D), Spiritual Practices, Levels of Consciousness, Journey of Soul, Twin Flames, Unconditional Love, Jo Conrad Interview with Omnec Onec.

"I am certain today that I have incarnated as one of the souls to break down encrusted structures and to help both myself and

people to allow true, divine love to rise and to embody. We are here to help Mother Earth to ascend to a higher vibrational frequency and to end the age of darkness and ignorance."
Anja Schäfer – venus-spirit.com
New Release 2023, DISCUS Publishing
ISBN: 978-3-910804-02-9

Venus Historian Dr. Raymond Keller

Dr. Raymond Andrew Keller aka "Cosmic Ray" is the Historian of the Venusians, contactee, UFO researcher, author and retired Doctor of History. Ray's VENUS RISING book series explores numerous facets of Venus. Well documented and based on personal research and years of experience, Ray's books reveal amazing connections from the perspectives of history, mythology, theosophy, space exploration, ufology, contactees, Venusians, spirituality, and current events.

Venus Rising – A Concise History of the Second Planet, 2016
The Final Countdown: Rockets to Venus, 2018
Cosmic Rays Excellent Venus Adventure, 2018
The Vast Venus Conspiracy, 2021

Lady Columba Venus Revelations, 2021
Flying Saucers and the Venus Legacy, 2022
From Venus They Come, 2022
Book 1 to 7 published by Headline Books, WV, USA *https://headlinebooks.com/* in cooperation with Dr. Keller.
More about Cosmic Ray: *https://venus-spirit.com/ray*

The Gospels of Thomas and Mary Magdalene
Dr. Raymond Keller
This Gospel of Thomas, inclusive of the Gospel of Mary Magdalene, was found at the Nag Hammadi site in the Egyptian desert in December of 1945 along with some other books collectively called the "Nag Hammadi Library." These texts were very fragmented with age and in a state of advanced decay. The original parchments now rest in the Coptic Museum in Cairo. They have been thought to have been written and dated from 100-245 A.D., according to some sources.

Until today these sacred texts have only been able to be partially interpreted by scholars because no complete record of these texts has ever been found. That these texts are even real is debated by many. It is possible, but doubtful, that these texts are in their complete form anywhere in the world, not even in the library beneath the Vatican. Even if these texts were there, they could not be as complete or as accurate as this version for this edition is a supernatural gift to the faithful through the Hierarchy of Light.

2022, DISCUS Publishing
ISBN: 978-3-9817441-9-4

CDs from Omnec Onec

In collaboration with the music producer Wulf Wemmje, Omnec Onec created these three beautiful CDs under Venusian inspiration.

Soul Journey
Guided Meditation with various music compositions corresponding to the levels of consciousness. Mantras and visualizations support the experience of the different dimensions from the physical through the astral, the causal, and the etheric dimension to the God planes. *"The Soul Travel technique enables you to leave the physical body withouth the connection of the silver chord. You travel with light and sound and have access to any dimension you wish, where you can gain knowledge or make an experience for the benefit of Soul while still existing in the physical."*

My Mission on Earth
Omnec tells the story of her origin and shares universal knowledge
Listen to Omnec's fascinating voice, embedded in sound spheres and Venusian inspired music, how she describes in her own words the connection of Venus to the history of the Earth and the purpose and goal of her adventurous transfer from the astral plane to the physical Earth.

From Venus with Love

Omnec speaks and sings about love with spherical background music. "Love in the physical realm is one of the most powerful emotions, that is expressed in unlimited ways. Love can overwhelm the senses, or love can be subtle. Love is different for each of us. Love can be used to create, or love can destroy. Love can be used to manipulate and control, or love can be given freely. Love can make you a prisoner, and love can make you free. Once you have experienced love in all forms, then you get to know unconditional love. Venus Love is unconditional love." (Omnec Onec, Introduction CD "From Venus with Love")

The CDs are available physically and as downloads in our **Venus Spirit Online-Shop https://venus-spirit.com. Here,** you can also enjoy audio samples.

Contact

Anja Schäfer

Venus Spirit Website: https://venus-spirit.com

Omnec Onec Website: https://omnec-onec.com

Venus Spirit YouTube Channel:
https://www.youtube.com/@venus-spirit

Please subscribe to our Venus Spirit Newsletter.

Let's connect more and more with each other and create an amazing new Earth together!

May the Universal Love and Blessings Be

Anja ♥

Made in the USA
Middletown, DE
23 September 2023

39158478R00076